SURVIVING THE SHADOWS

CAROLINE WHITEHEAD

Agio
PUBLISHING HOUSE

151 Howe Street, Victoria BC Canada V8V 4K5

*For rights information and bulk orders, please
contact:* info@agiopublishing.com *or go to*
www.agiopublishing.com

Surviving The Shadows
ISBN 978-1-897435-33-5 (trade paperback)
Cataloguing information available from
Library and Archives Canada

Printed on acid-free paper that includes no fibre from
endangered forests. Agio Publishing House is a socially responsible
company, measuring success on a triple-bottom-line basis.

10   9   8   7   6   5   4   3   2   1

To my daughter Caroline and family.
Love endureth all things.

ACKNOWLEDGEMENTS

First and foremost, my grateful thanks and appreciation to the late Angus Baxter, a well-known genealogist, who gave me years of invaluable advice, and encouragement, on how to go about obtaining family records.

To Miss Joan Coburn, Head Archivist of the Greater London Record Office and Library, for assisting with the background details of my early childhood and birth record.

To Mr. D. Allen, Record Officer of the Ministry of Defence, Hayes, Middlesex, for his time and on-going support when searching the Naval records.

To Mr. P. Rudall, of St. Catherine's House, London, who agreed to do a ten-year search on my parents, and provided me with important family documents.

The Folkestone Library, Kent, for supplying me with information on the 1928 Court Order proceedings relating to family members.

The London Office of the Salvation Army for their invaluable help in tracing family.

This book could not have been compiled but for the generous help and co-operation from those offices above, connected with family history.

My gratitude to Bruce and Marsha Batchelor of Agio Publishing House for their support and expertise.

And to my dear brother Rowland, who gave endless support, encouragement and love to me during a difficult time.

Thank you.

ABOUT THE BOOK

This is the true story of a young girl brought up in the strict and harsh life of a Catholic orphanage in the aftermath of the First World War, and of her struggle for emotional survival.

Told by the nuns she was an orphan, she set out to search for her roots – an overwhelming desire within her forced her onward, if only to prove the nuns wrong.

Her perilous journeys through war-torn London, and monumental struggle against the Catholic authorities in her search for kith and kin, lasted over forty years. As the years rolled by, her search for family became a way of life, even after emigrating to Canada in 1967. Her determination and spirit urged her to make the pilgrimage back to the land of her birth, every other year, with little success.

But for the kindness of the late Angus Baxter, a genealogist who lived in Lakefield, Ontario, those tightly-held archive doors may have been forever closed. With his help, they were now unbolted and the mysteries began to unravel one bizarre piece at a time. Reaching her early sixties, and in possession of valuable information through Angus Baxter who was unable to help her further, she hired the services of David Wright, a researcher living in Whitstable in the County of Kent. In 1990, she received news from him that her parents, whom she had spent a lifetime searching for, had passed on.

Further details from Mr. Wright sent shock waves through her, leaving her speechless in disbelief. While searching the records he found the birth certificate of an elder brother who was unknown to her. Born in 1919, he would be seventy-two years of age at the time. Was it possible that, by some miracle, he was still alive?

THE SEARCH BEGINS

B y the time I reached sixteen years of age, I had spent all but two years of my young life in the somewhat questionable care of nuns at an orphanage in a small village in the County of Kent, England. From there, I was sent "out into the world" of which I knew little or nothing about, and had not even been prepared for. Having no choice whatsoever, I was put into domestic service and remained in that position for eighteen months. My first place of employment was a reformatory school for unruly boys staffed by Christian Brothers, some of whom seemed intent on breaking their vows of chastity.

With the outbreak of World War II, owing to an order from the British Parliament that all young people over the age of sixteen must report to the nearest Labour Exchange for essential war work, I managed to extricate myself as quickly as possible from domestic service – realizing this golden opportunity to escape servile work could not be missed.

Giving me a train voucher, an office clerk at the Labour Exchange in Banstead, County of Surrey, told me to report for work at an aircraft factory in Weybridge, Surrey, where I would be forced to stay until hostilities ended.

In July 1944, a few months after my marriage, I was seized by a compulsive urge to trace the whereabouts of my parents whom I understood had lived in London at the time of my birth. During this period the Second World War – now in its fifth year – battled on in Europe, causing chaos with the lives of all people. Rationing and food shortages in Britain made life intolerable for everyone and, although most of the people were willing to help their country in every possible way, the toughest part of surviving, for many, was to stay alive and keep oneself from freezing from the cold. This was by no means an easy task, as coal or any other form of heating was in short supply and this caused many hardships during the extremely cold winters of the 1940s. I remember wearing a pair of men's old, thick socks in bed and knitted woollen gloves with the fingers cut off, that had seen better days, which I had found by sheer luck – a luxury I silently guarded.

It didn't dawn on me at that time the hurdles I would have to cross in the search for my parents, nor the risks I would have to take. The train that travelled from Walton-on-Thames in the County of Surrey to London, on the Aldershot, Hampshire line, was always jammed-packed with soldiers, and was an on-going target during the bombings. A main concern was to get to London as quickly as possible and, hopefully, in one piece. However, if a bomb landed near any of the railway lines during the journey, the train would come to a shrieking halt, scattering passengers everywhere.

Once over the shock, heads would peer out of the train windows to see at which station the train had stopped. What surprised most travellers, though, was how quickly the railway lines were cleared of debris when a bomb fell, and how little behind schedule the train was when reaching its destination. Although I travelled the line from Walton-on-Thames to Waterloo in London, many times, I was always horrified to see en route the destruction of homes, indeed entire streets, caused by these bombings.

It was during one such trip, armed with the only information I possessed – a piece of paper showing the place of my baptism – I began the search for my parents. I knew that I had been baptized in the Roman Catholic Church of The English Martyrs at Walworth in the East End of London, but wasn't quite sure how to get there from Waterloo station. After making several inquiries to passers-by, I was told to catch a certain bus that would put me down within a five minute walk to the church.

When arriving at the church I noticed the priests' house was close by, so I approached the front door and knocked on it. As the door slowly opened, a slender, young priest was standing inside. Asking if there was anything he could do for me, I explained to him briefly the reason for my unannounced visit and questioned if it was possible to have the parish records checked in order to confirm the accuracy of my baptism record.

Inviting me into a small library, the priest took down from a bookshelf a large black binder covering religious ceremonies that were held in the mid-1920s, and studied it carefully. After checking the records for a few minutes, he told me he couldn't find any entry of my parents as having been parishioners at his church. Neither could he enlighten me as to my parents' identity or whereabouts. Thanking the priest for his help, and leaving a small donation on the table, I left the library feeling this was not a good beginning and that, perhaps, I had wasted my journey.

Mulling over my thoughts while homeward-bound to Surrey I decided the next course of action would be to obtain a copy of my birth certificate at the earliest opportunity.

On a bright sunny morning, I took the train from Walton-on-Thames railway station and travelled to Somerset House in London, where all births, marriages and death certificates are recorded.

Upon arriving, I went over to one of the enquiry windows and asked the clerk how I would go about obtaining a birth certificate. Handing me an official application form, she told me to fill in all my details. Looking at the form with some apprehension, uncertain as to how I would go about giving information of which I had scant knowledge, I filled in my name, date of birth. Duly completed, together with the required fee, I handed the form back to the clerk, who advised me the certificate would be forwarded by mail, within two or three weeks.

After waiting impatiently for the document, the day finally arrived mid-week when an official-looking brown envelope was pushed through the letterbox of my front door. Excited, I picked it up off the mat, ran up the staircase two steps at a time, to the quiet of my bedroom, closed the door, and sat down on the double bed. With shaking fingers I tore open the envelope, fearful of what secrets it held, and glued my eyes to the document.

Scrutinizing and absorbing every detail, I learned my parents' full names and where they had lived at the time of my birth. I also learned my true name was Caroline and not Carrie, which everyone at the orphanage had called me throughout my childhood. One thing, firmly established: I was a Londoner. Carefully folding the document and returning it inside the envelope, I slid it for safe-keeping beneath some lingerie in one of my dressing table drawers. With the information I now obtained of where my parents lived in 1925, the thought of finding them and actually seeing them, excited me. It seemed worth searching this area first.

The following Monday morning, with no rain clouds in sight, I rose early in order to have sufficient time to dress leisurely. Determined to create a good impression on my parents, I put on my one and only two-piece suit, which I reserved for special occasions. It was patterned in small checks, in colours of grey and mauve. Using sparse make-up, and taking a last look at the mirror, I assured myself that my appearance would meet with their approval.

Mimicking a businessman's attire, I took from the wardrobe a rolled-up umbrella, also grey, which blended well with my outfit and gave me, I thought, an air of distinction. Using my umbrella as a walking stick, I wended my way to Walton-on-Thames railway station and mingled with the early morning business crowd on the platform. Looking well-groomed and feeling somewhat smug, there were no doubts in my mind that I would, and always would, rise to the occasion like anyone else, when needed.

Boarding the Waterloo train to London, I took a seat close to the window. As I sat watching the landscape flashing by, endless questions raced through my head at a speed which equalled that of the train as it charged from one station to the next. I wondered what my parents looked like, and how they would react when told I was their daughter. Would they accept me or simply deny all knowledge of my existence, thereby closing the door? Perhaps an embarrassment of their painful past, now anxious to catch up with them, would indicate a wish to disown me. Nevertheless, to all these questions, it was a chance I was prepared to take, whatever the consequence.

I was impatient for the train to arrive, yet at the same time I experienced a feeling of unease about my first visit to parents whom I had never known. Perhaps I should have written, beforehand, a letter of my intended visit, rather than appearing out of the blue on their front doorstep. As the train crawled into Waterloo railway station, I felt compelled to go on.

Leaving the station and noting the Parliament Buildings on the right, I turned left and walked under a railway bridge. This led me into Westminster Bridge Road, the address shown on my birth certificate. I began checking the house numbers, my heart thumping, looking for No. 72.

Walking less than ten minutes, the houses suddenly seemed to disappear; No. 72 was nowhere in sight. Looking around, I wondered what to do next as all I could see on the ground was a large, solid block of concrete. Staring hard at it for a second or two I surmised I had turned, unknowingly, from Westminster Bridge Road into another road – and was about to walk away from the block when a worker, wearing a grubby cloth cap, walked towards me. I asked him if he knew where No. 72 house was, and told him I was trying to find my parents.

Giving me a puzzled look, and without hesitation, he said, 'You're standing on it, ducks; bloody bombs blew 'em all up.'

Speechless, I continued staring at the concrete block, feeling thoroughly miserable that my efforts to find my parents had failed.

Finally gathering my senses, and determined not to let this minor setback get the better of me, I began to search next for No. 182 Westmoreland Road, Walworth, in the East End of London – the place of my birth.

Taking the advice of the worker to go on the underground train to Stoke Newington, within a short space of time I found myself walking along Westmoreland Road. Again, checking house numbers, I walked until reaching a long, high brick wall, at the end of which a large brick building came into view. It was No. 182. Thinking this to be surely a mistake since I had come looking for a house and not a large building, I stopped a man in the street and asked if this was the correct address.

Assuring me it was, he said, 'Why don't you go into reception and ask to see the Warden? I'm sure he can help you.'

I thought I had missed the point, and couldn't grasp the reason why I needed to see a Warden. Mumbling my thanks to the passer-by I was undecided whether to enter or run from the building. It was a formidable-looking place and my intuition that the building was some sort of institution, gave me an uncomfortable feeling – as if I was again entering an orphanage or other ominous place. Just looking at it put the fear of God into me. I felt I was about to enter the confessional box and expose my very soul.

"Truth Conquers" are words I have often heard. The truth of the matter now, was that I would never be satisfied until I knew the whole truth about myself and my parents. Convincing myself there was nothing to be afraid of, I slowly entered the building.

Approaching the clerk at the reception desk, I asked to see the person-in-charge. Offering me a seat, the young lady said, 'I'll ring and see if he's in his office.'

I waited but a few minutes, when a quietly-spoken gentleman came to where I sat and introduced himself as Mr. Hewitt, the Warden. He was a slim man in his early fifties, with thinning, light brown hair. What struck me quite noticeably about Mr. Hewitt was not his elegant clothes or his equally elegant manners, but the majestic smile on his unlined benign face, and his small, friendly eyes which positively twinkled. He looked a "Divine Being". I stared at him fascinated. Although realizing he was a person of authority, I felt confident he could be entrusted with the burden of my somewhat embarrassing enquiries and I would have no qualms in talking to him about them.

Inviting me into his small office, we sat facing each other across a large oak desk on which sat stacks of papers. Asking me what he could do to help, I showed him the details of my birth certificate and asked if he held any records showing my entry into the world. Leaving his chair, he went over to a bookshelf and took from it a large, black volume. Checking the year 1925, he read out the entry – date: September 25, time: 7.15 p.m. – confirming aloud that my mother had indeed been admitted to the institution and gave birth to me on that date.

My face, no longer smug, fell flat when hearing this appalling news. It wasn't what I wanted to hear.

Noting my crestfallen look, Mr. Hewitt continued, as though to cheer me up, 'You weren't the only child born here, you know. There were thousands of poor women who needed somewhere to go to have their babies, and this is where they came.'

I couldn't respond to this half-cheery statement, nor minimize the hurt I felt in learning I was born in this institution. Totally depressed by the thought of it, I was determined never in my life to divulge this miserable secret to anyone.

Questioning Mr. Hewitt of any knowledge of my parents' whereabouts, he responded that, regrettably, he didn't know. He knew the area where they had lived quite well but with all the bombings that went on in London during the war, the majority of the people had scattered to other parts of the country. Perhaps they, too, had evacuated.

Before leaving his office I questioned Mr. Hewitt about the building. He explained that the old institution was now a Geriatric Home for the Aged and was known as 'Newington Lodge'.

Apologizing for not being able to help further, Mr. Hewitt shook my hand, wished me better luck in the search of my family, and added, 'They would be proud of you.'

THE ORPHANAGE

On the return journey to Walton-on-Thames, my thoughts trailed from Walworth, London, to Orpington in the County of Kent. It was here in this tiny village that I spent my childhood years – from 1927 to 1941 – living in an institution known as St. Anne's. As a child I lived in fear of those in charge, knowing their eyes were constantly watching me. If she heard the slightest noise, a shaft of light from the nun's cubicle would cast shadows in every corner of the dormitory. Silent figures, shuffling along in slippered feet, carrying a lighted candle, would glide from bed to bed to see if each child was asleep. The very presence of a nun approaching a sleepless child's bed would cause the child to lie there paralyzed, trembling with fright.

How did I get to St. Anne's? Decades later, I would learn that, on November 5 1927, at two years of age, having been abandoned by my mother in a shop doorway and taken by an unknown person to Carter Street Police Station in London, I was admitted into St. Anne's Orphanage, a large ugly-looking brick building with lots and lots of windows that looked out onto lawns. The orphanage was situated approximately twenty miles south of London and run by the Sisters of Mercy nuns, whose headquarters were located at Bermondsey.

An Irish woman, Catherine McAuley, who was over fifty years of age when she became a nun, was the foundress of the Sisters of Mercy. She was born into a middle-class family in north County Dublin and in her mid-twenties she took orphans into her home and helped the poor of her area. Later known as Mother M. Catherine McAuley, she opened her first House in Britain at Bermondsey, East London in 1839.

Sadly, her concept of caring for orphaned children turned into the opposite of what she had envisaged, at least for the children who were put into the care of St. Anne's. Because of the harsh treatment imposed upon the children and lack of caring, I feel she would have strongly disapproved.

I was promptly nicknamed "Carrie", perhaps because the nuns thought the name Caroline sounded too sophisticated for a ragamuffin like me, born in a London workhouse.

Much of my early life at the orphanage is a blur; however, I've been told that when arriving there, a strange lady took me by the hand and put me into large quarters known as "The Nursery", which was the Receiving Home for new children. These quarters accommodated about twelve or more babies and toddlers who were cared for by the nuns and their staff. The nursery was separated from the main building of St. Anne's by a long, gravel pathway, flanked on both sides by privet hedges.

Situated at the top of the pathway was the Holy Innocents church, built in 1909 through the generosity of an anonymous donor. To the right of the church was St. Anne's and to the left of the church was St. Joseph's, which housed boys from many poverty-stricken areas of London.

The building of St. Joseph's orphanage for 200 boys from the age of four upward, was completed in 1892. In July 1893, the Presentation Brothers arrived from Cork, Ireland, to begin their work of teaching and educating the boys. Typical early arrivals were James McCarthy, aged ten, from the parish of St. Olave's, London, having spent the previous two years in the workhouse; and John Gorman, aged eleven, from the parish of Lambeth, London, where he had spent four years in a workhouse.

Both St. Anne's and St. Joseph's were under the auspices of the Catholic Children's Rescue Society, and Southwark Diocese, whose headquarters are located at Westminster Bridge Road, London.

On the upper floor of the nursery were two little dormitories equipped with cots, a large bathroom, and sleeping quarters for the resident nun. The staff quarters were in another house, adjoining the nursery. The lower floor consisted of a dining-room with tiny tables and chairs, a kitchen, and a playroom with lots of toys and a small play slide.

Weather permitting, the children would play outside on the slides

Above Left: *An aerial view with St. Joseph's at left, Holy Innocents church in centre, and St. Anne's Orphanage at right.* Top: *The dormitory wing of St. Anne's Orphanage as seen from the bottom of the Avenue.*

Below: *Four of the girls on the Avenue, with St. Joseph's in the background, and Holy Innocents church at right.*

and swings, under the watchful eyes of the nuns or staff. On most days, especially Sundays and feast days, the toddlers were taken for walks up the long pathway leading to the church, and taken inside to say a few prayers.

The staff, mainly young girls training to be nursery nurses, didn't stay too long at the nursery; they came and went like flies. This was in all probability due to the nun-in-charge, Sister Ethelreda, who constantly screamed at the top of her lungs, terrorizing everyone who came within inches of her. Not only did she run the nursery with an iron rod, but also the infirmary. However, it must be said that in fairness to her strong character, she was excellent in treating the children's health problems.

Although the babies and toddlers were reasonably well looked after, I was sadly aware of the lack of love they received. Indeed, I was witness to many cruelties. On one occasion, a tiny boy had wet his cot and a nurse, whose name I have long forgotten, pulled the wet sheet out from under him and beat him soundly across the legs. I was so mortified and frightened by this dreadful scene, I turned and ran crying bitterly out of the nursery and up the long pathway into the sanctuary of the church.

'Please God,' I prayed, 'protect the children.'

Looking up at the outstretched arms of the Sacred Heart of Jesus, above the altar, I puzzled how God could allow such cruelty in His midst. Sad to say no one, not even myself, would ever think of speaking to the Mother Superior about what you witnessed, heard or felt; you simply held all your emotions tightly within and locked the secrets away, hoping that one day circumstances would change.

The nursery was to be my home until I reached the age of four, when I was then transferred to join the older girls in the main building of the orphanage and to begin my schooling. The school was within the perimeter of the children's playground and playing fields. The girls, in later years, actively participated in netball and field hockey in these areas. These games were thoroughly enjoyed by everyone, enabling us to expend our excess energies which, otherwise, were strictly suppressed.

Although some of the nuns who cared for the girls under their charge were kind, most of them routinely strapped or caned us for little or no apparent reason. We often wondered why they were called "Sisters of

Mercy", because to the girls they showed not the slightest mercy, especially when exercising discipline. Ear and hair pulling went on constantly, and the dread of the stinging cane can never be forgotten.

I remember clearly on one occasion, when only a youngster, accidentally dropping a water glass in the refectory. I froze to the spot, petrified!

Caught by the scruff of the neck by the nun-in-charge, Sister Kevin, I was told to 'Go to the pantry broom cupboard, fetch a pan and brush, and clean up the mess.' She then added, 'And when you've finished, girl, go and stand in the corner of the scullery and wait for me.'

A few minutes later she entered the scullery holding an evil-looking cane in her hand. Looking at the cane, and knowing what was to come, I began shaking all over. Thoroughly preaching the pros and cons on being sinful, she administered three strokes of the cane on each hand.

While tears fell down my cheeks, and holding my sore hands, the nun told me I was to pay for the cost of the water glass, which would be tuppence. I had no idea what tuppence looked like, or how I would find it. Would God in His wisdom make the nun forget about the incident, I wondered? I never did pay for the broken glass.

A gathering at Dymchurch in 1938. Sister Kevin and Bishop Healey and a group of the girls. The author is to the left of Sister Kevin.

Growing up in the orphanage was much the same for me as for the rest of the girls. We all dressed alike in the same navy blue serge uniforms in the winter, and in the summer wore identical striped frocks; all clothing was numbered, as you would identify prisoners. We ate the same sparse, dull meals, mainly stews, with two boiled eggs a year, one at Christmas and one at Easter. Everyone had the same distinctive convent-style haircut, cropped above the ears.

My light brown, naturally wavy hair would grow into rolls of curls of which I was quite proud. A sin in itself. To my dismay, however, the nun who looked after the girls' hair grooming saw fit to take up a pair of heavy shearing scissors and cut the curls off, one by one. Needless to say, this action wounded my pride and, when seeing the curls fall onto the floor, tears streamed down my face.

If a girl arrived at the orphanage at an early age as I had, she was transferred from the nursery to the infants' classroom and was taught the rudiments of early curriculum by a Scottish lady named Miss Murray, who also served as the music teacher. Miss Murray was a spinster, somewhat bland and stoutly, and of medium height. She wore her black hair in a style typical of the roaring twenties, but she couldn't be described as a "flapper" in any sense of the word as her body movements were anything but supple.

Each year at Christmas time, Miss Murray would organize the Christmas plays. A chosen few handpicked girls played out scenes from The Nativity before an audience of nuns, priests, staff, girls and visitors who included parishioners from the church. Sometimes I was chosen to play an angel, and was costumed in a white dress with transparent wings. Loudly, I would sing 'Away in a Manger', to my heart's content, totally carried away by the thought that I was floating upward to heaven. So oblivious to what was happening, on stage, I'd suddenly get a shove from one of the other players telling me to, 'Get on with it!'

Every year the play was a success. Whatever flaws there were went unnoticed, and the stage settings and costumes got better and better. Our excitement of the day was that acting before dignitaries made us feel important. Also, while normally forbidden, the players were allowed to use lipstick, face powder and rouge on their cheeks for these occasions. This was made available to us by some of the working staff. To dream of washing off the make-up after the play would be tantamount to sacrilege; we would try making it last on our faces for days, hoping our "importance" never wore off.

Catechism was the first priority lesson of the school day. The lessons and prayers of the Mass were taken in Latin by the head mistress, Sister Attracta, or Father Fitzmorris, one of the priests belonging to the Holy Innocents church. What a delightful man he was; tall, slender, of delicate features and quietly-spoken, he had endless patience with any of the girls who couldn't quite master the art of speaking in Latin. It was a sad time for everyone when God 'took him' early in his young life, and we mourned the loss. He was buried in the little cemetery, close by the playing fields.

All children who came into the orphanage with "questionable" baptismal records were immediately "conditionally" baptized by the parish priest, with a staff member of the orphanage "standing in" as Godparent.

The girls were prepared for their First Holy Communion around the age of five or six, and confirmed into the Catholic faith by the time they reached seven years. Birthdays were never celebrated at St. Anne's as the majority of the girls hardly knew the date on which they were born. The old saying, 'what you don't know, you won't miss,' certainly applied in this instance.

Church was a "must" on all holy days, and we were obliged to get up at the crack of dawn to attend mass.

Masses were also attended twice on Sundays, early and mid-morning, as well as evening Benediction. All services were spoken or sung in Latin and we chanted in parrot-style fashion our responses to the serving priest. The magnificent voices of the choir intensified the solemnity of the service, and the singing of the hymns brought me a measure of peace. Singing also provided me with the opportunity of exercising my voice box, for normally, when spoken to, we girls responded in whispered, meek voices. This lack of voice projection affected me greatly in my early adult life as I tended to "croak" out my words; this was not only embarrassing to me, but was annoying to the listener. I was forever being told to 'speak up.'

The joy of celebrating a feast day was made more enjoyable by the Mother Superior, who lined up the girls in the playground and, from a pail filled with sweets, would diligently dole out a few into each girl's small hand. Savouring one sweet at a time, I would wrap up the rest of them in a piece of toilet paper or anything else I could find, and hide them in my own secret hiding place unknown to anyone else. Imagine how shocked I was, when returning one day to retrieve the remainder of the sweets, to find them all gone! Some hungry little thief had pinched them and devoured the lot, and I never did discover who she was.

By the time I reached eight years of age, I had developed much skill in the art of needlework and knitting and, on several occasions, my work was entered into competitions held by the Arts and Crafts Guild

Sister Attracta, who was Headmistress, with a knitting class.

of London. Exquisite smocking, hand-stitched on the bodice of a pure, green silk baby's dress, won me a prize. However I never received the money order or achievement certificate, that was due me.

It was during this period in my life that a staff member, herself an "old girl", told me that I had a younger sister, Elizabeth, and an older sister, Margaret, living in the same orphanage. This information didn't convey much meaning to me at the time and my response to this piece of news was somewhat negative.

She collected us all together in the playground and, pointing a finger at each of us, said, 'You, you and you, are all sisters.'

Margaret was about twelve years old, with light brown, wavy hair, cut short at the ears. She looked very tall compared to me. Elizabeth was six and had dark brown, straight hair, and a chubby, little face. I cannot remember feeling any particular emotion on meeting my sisters for the first time; we simply stood staring at each other, then walked away to play with our own friends.

Having a sister, what did it mean? I'd been so completely deprived of a "normal" childhood that I had no concept of how to relate to real family members.

We were also told by the same staff member that a brother of ours was living in a boys' home at Gravesend in the County of Kent, not too far away. It would be years before any of us were to meet him and learn his name was William.

Soon afterwards, my sister Margaret, until now known at St. Anne's as Kathleen Brandon, had her surname changed by the nuns to Marshall. Unbeknownst to us, in 1932, when my older brother Rowland was removed from St. Joseph's, Littlehampton, and taken home by our mother, his name was also changed from Brandon to Marshall.

What was going on? The name changes were disorienting – who were we really?

Decades later, on one of my visits to England, I arranged to visit archivist Mr. Lyons at Purley, Surrey, specifically to ask him if he could

Above: *Elizabeth, Margaret and Carrie in 1933.*
We'd just been told we were sisters!

Below: *Carrie and Elizabeth paddling at Dymchurch in 1933.*
None of us could swim – hence the rubber ring.

check St. Anne's register to find out when and why my sister's name changed from Brandon to Marshall. No entry could be found.

The nuns never spoke to us about our parents or relatives regardless of whether they had knowledge of them or not; their general attitude was one of indifference. Perhaps in the mid-twenties or thirties it was the "silent" rule. Many times, when some of the girls had parents visiting once or twice a month, I would wonder why I didn't have the same privilege. If I had siblings, perhaps, I had living parents somewhere. What also puzzled me was that if these girls had mothers and fathers, why were they at St. Anne's orphanage? The only parents I knew were the Mother Superior and Parish Priest, whom everyone respectfully called, 'Mother' and 'Father'. No one ever came to visit me.

My fondest memories of the St. Anne's girls was their profound loyalty to each other. It was a silent code never to "snitch" on one another despite the threat of questioning or caning. If a girl got walloped by either nun or staff, the other girls would rally round and comfort the victim as best as possible, offering as compensation the last sweet if you had one, or an old rag doll you made and treasured.

Not an exceptional student at school, I found it "hard graft" coping with some of the subjects, in particular, maths. The subjects I enjoyed most were literature, history, music, arts and science and sports. Netball and field hockey I played with much enthusiasm and, excelling at netball, was chosen to play in many teams both at home and away at different schools and convents in London. It was always a thrill to be able to travel with the team and Sports Mistress by train to London, and then indulge in the delicious teas served after the match.

During my years at the orphanage, Mother Marcellina, the Superior, was the one nun whom I truly loved and respected. To me, she was the "Mother" of all mothers, and this feeling probably came about because she was always kind to all of us. Of medium height, she walked with an air of authority that made one realize she definitely was in charge. Her rosy cheeks and soft complexion gave her a healthy glow; her eyes never stopped smiling. Always scurrying here, there and everywhere in the endless corridors or playground, her long black habit literally "took off" in the wind and her feet almost left the ground.

Whenever she was entering the playground – having carefully reached the last concrete step down to the ground – the children, as though appearing out of nowhere, would swamp her in greetings of love and affection. She always picked up the smallest child in the crowd, stroked her hair and kissed her, but her arms reached out to us all. She seldom reprimanded any girl unless it was something very serious.

Her punishments were usually in the form of prayers; for instance, kneeling down on the cold, marble floor under the big clock, at the top of the marble corridor, and made to say six or more Hail Mary's, with probably a Confiteor thrown in. The loud ticking of the clock always unnerved me as I felt it was sending out an ominous warning that if I didn't repent, I would surely go to Hell. The greatest embarrassment of standing under the clock was that everyone passing knew why you were standing or kneeling there. But, never a word was spoken.

This punishment was metered out to me twice – once when I was swinging merrily on the curtain rod in the bathroom area and it came crashing down, taking most of the plaster off the wall with it; the other time when I went up to the playing field with several girls to swing on the maypole.

On this bright, sunny day, with not a cloud in the sky, we were oblivious to the fact that we were totally out of bounds and without permission of either nun or staff. The big iron rings, attached to each end of the long chains from the centre of the maypole, used to leave rust marks on the hands and were hard to hold onto. I decided to tuck up the bottom part of my summer frock and put it through the ring, holding on only to the material.

A girl gave us a "starter" push, grabbed the remaining empty swinging ring and off we went, feet off the ground, flying higher and higher. We were all laughing, having a great time, when suddenly the material on my frock gave way and I was on my own, flying like a trapeze artist, over the swings and slides, and landed on the other side of the field.

Picking myself up, I felt somewhat shaken, but was glad of no broken bones and was unconcerned with the scratches and bruising on my arms and legs. What did concern me, though, was how I was going to account for my torn frock, now minus its bottom half. The frightening task was in reporting the damage to the workroom. We all came down from the playing field together, with the girls flanking me so that no one of authority would see the state of my frock.

We walked toward the workroom and on reaching the door, one of the girls opened it and shoved me in. I thought I would be sick!

Sheepishly approaching May Lyle, the school seamstress and person in charge of the workroom, I showed her my frock, holding the torn piece of material in my hand. She looked at me, unbelievingly, and her brown eyes got bigger and bigger.

Shaking her finger within inches of my nose, she scolded, 'You wicked child, what have you done? Take off that frock.'

She handed me a pair of scissors, adding, 'Cut off the buttons and put them in the button box, and put that filthy torn frock into the rag bag.'

While standing in my underclothes, I was then given a clean frock and told: 'Now, go and stand under the clock and wait for Mother. Woe betide you, girl, if you ever do that again.'

The ordeal over, I reasoned to myself that I had got off lightly. I had half-expected a short, sharp clip around the head but mercifully, it was not forthcoming. May Lyle's nimble fingers would produce the most exquisite needlework; she was a marvel at it and every piece perfect – but if she used her strong hands to administer a wallop it could send you spinning across the workroom floor.

May Lyle taught many girls the art of cutting fabric on the bias, how to make clothes and how to knit socks on four needles. From an early age the girls were made to repair their own socks, and we sat on wooden benches in the workroom laboriously repairing the work at hand, which was carried out in complete silence, as we were not allowed to speak to each other. If you did a poor job of repairing, and it was not up to May Lyle's standard, she would take her big shearing scissors, cutting out all the stitches, and make you do it all over again. A number of the girls would end up crying. But tears, no matter how bitterly shed, made no impression upon May Lyle; you did the task, even if it took all day.

There were always two rag bags kept in the workroom. One held the odd pieces of new material that came off the large rolls of fabric from which the girl's clothes were made. The other bag held odd bits of linen or clothing no longer repairable and these were used for cleaning purposes around the orphanage. When May Lyle was in a generous mood, and a girl asked her for odd pieces of material from one of the rag bags, she allowed you to take from it whatever you wanted. When making a rag doll, however, it usually ended up looking like a dressed clown, as all the arms, legs and body were made from differently textured and coloured materials: green, pink, blue, black and brown stripe. The doll's face was made from white sheeting and was stitched with strong, black thread to outline the features of the eyes, nose and mouth. Failing a thread, we used pencil.

I'm convinced that, although growing up from an innocent child, a nasty streak lurked somewhere inside me, as I took the greatest delight in putting my rag doll through purgatory when testing its stress performance. Attaching the head to the body with the strong, black thread, I would twist it around and around the neck until the head was held securely in place. With a final thrust of the needle into the neck, and pulling tightly on the thread, I would complete my creation with two good knots. Then, leaving the thread attached to the doll, I would swing it crazily into the air, admiring it from every angle. Finally, when completely satisfied with my creation, I would cut it loose from its "umbilical cord". These rag dolls were much treasured in our younger days and we only parted with them, reluctantly, to comfort another girl.

When I was very young, Miss Condon was in charge of the workroom and May Lyle was her assistant. The two ladies sat facing each other, using electric sewing machines that stood on a wooden platform. Miss Condon had a gaunt expression that permanently masked her grey face. Her hair, also grey, was worn at the back of her head in a neat bun, held in place with long pins. She had one leg, a mystery to all of us, and a wooden crutch which she kept by the side of her sewing machine. We nicknamed her "Old Wooden Leg".

She never moved off her chair from the time she sat down – instead, she would bang the crutch on the platform and demanded: 'Girl, come up here!'

If questioning the girl did not produce the correct response, Miss Condon's wooden crutch – like a flash of lightening – would catch you sharply across the legs. I was totally in awe of "Old Wooden Leg", and marvelled at the speed with which she could move, despite her disability.

One day, rumours ran riot throughout the playground that "Old Wooden Leg" was dead. Speculating how this came about and drawing no conclusion, the other girls carried on with their activities in the playground as though nothing had happened.

On this particular day I was in the workroom when May Lyle gave me the news that Miss Condon had passed away. She then asked if I would like to see her for one last time.

Rather taken aback, I muttered, 'Yes, Miss.'

We went up the staircase leading from the marble corridor, and walked along the upper floor to Miss Condon's bedroom. Upon reaching the bedroom door, May Lyle ushered me in.

Miss Condon was lying on the bed, with her arms folded across her chest; a bedspread had been placed over the lower part of her body. Her wooden crutch was nowhere in sight.

Never having seen a dead person before, I felt a bit scared and was deep in thought when May Lyle said, 'Doesn't she look peaceful.'

'Yes, Miss,' I replied.

After standing in silence for one minute, we paid our respects by saying one Hail Mary, for the saving of her soul, then crept silently out of the bedroom, gently closing the door, and went back downstairs into the workroom.

When I first became aware of May Lyle I noticed she had thick, white hair, and deep-set brown eyes. Of medium height, her chubby figure and motherly appearance gave her a look of one's grandmother. I noticed, also, that when she smiled, two small dimples appeared on her cheeks. She loved music and spent many hours in the workroom, long after the day's work was done, listening to her radio or gramophone records. Adept at sewing, she made many of the children's clothes and saved the Diocese thousands of pounds sterling in expenses. Whatever

May Lyle, our seamstress, with a group of girls.

she did, was to perfection; no stitches ever fell apart at the seam on any of the garments she made.

As a seamstress in charge of the workroom she was relentless in her task to ensure that the large rolls of cloth, cut on long oak tables, were correctly cut on the bias, to avoid waste, and that any minute pieces of fabric left over, were put to good use. The rag bags took the remaining slithers of cloth, for the girls to use when making rag dolls.

May Lyle was a devout Catholic. Daily, after eating her mid-day meal, she could be seen walking around the quadrangle in front of St. Anne's, beads in hand, saying her rosary. After walking a few circuits, perhaps not only to pray but also to exercise her limbs from sitting many hours during the day at her sewing machine, she would return to the workroom, refreshed, bodily and spiritually.

THE CUBBY HOLE AND OTHER MEMORIES

It was known to the girls as the cubby hole, a recess measuring no more than 3 feet deep by 4 feet wide with shelves on either side of the walls, where the children's shoes and sandals were stored. Upon leaving the workroom via the staircase entrance to the upper floor, on the right hand side of the wall was the cubby hole; to the left side was the boiler room. From two concrete steps up, opposite the boiler room, a door led out onto the front of the building. The maintenance man was the only person allowed to use this entrance, although from time to time the girls would peek out of the door as if contemplating escape.

Maggie Walsh, a staff member, was in charge of distributing the footwear to the children. Tall, slender, with black curly hair, she seldom smiled and appeared to carry the world's problems on her shoulders. If the day didn't go in her favour, she was given to erratic moods. Perhaps the reason was that she had lost her mother. That her father, Farmer Walsh, worked for St. Joseph's presented her with the opportunity of residing and taking up work at St. Anne's, where she was allowed to visit with her father from time to time. She may have resented the fact this situation was not from choice, but necessity.

The long gravel pathway leading from the Nursery to the Holy Innocents church was flanked on either side by privet hedges. Over and beyond the other side of those hedges, half-way down the pathway to the left, was a large iron gate that opened and clanged shut, allowing Farmer Walsh, his horse and cart to enter and tend to the abundant rows of growing vegetables, as well as cultivate several apple trees.

Farmer Walsh's face had a glowing tan, and was lined and craggy, no doubt to being out in all weathers. A tall, slender man, who looked to be in his mid-fifties, he sported a walrus moustache, drooping down to his chin. He adored the St. Anne's girls. We would watch him in his horse cart, wearing typical farming clothes and an old battered hat that had seen better days. But beneath this hat was a happy, contented man.

If he thought it safe to do so without prying eyes, he would allow one or two girls, going up the gravel pathway, to hop aboard his horse cart and take us as close to the church as possible. Always chatting, with a smile beaming from ear to ear, his eyes twinkling, he would sometimes pop an apple into a child's hand. We loved this gentle man of a farmer whose countenance never changed from day to day, and was kind to everyone.

On the other hand, Maggie, his daughter, appeared a different character. She was very short on patience and, if a girl didn't respond quickly, would lash out at her.

When Miss Condon passed away, Maggie took over some of her responsibilities and assisted May Lyle in the workroom, repairing and making clothes, as well as looking after the children's footwear, stored in the cubby hole. There was a noticeable rapport between May Lyle and Maggie, and the girls wondered if this came about because of Maggie's domestic situation.

St. Joseph's not only provided St. Anne's with farm produce, crates of fresh milk and freshly-baked bread, but also repaired the girl's shoes. The quality of this workmanship was second to none, the best leather used. The sacks of footwear were delivered by one of the boys at the tradesman's entrance, at the side door. The sacks were picked up by one of the older girls and taken to Maggie Walsh in the workroom who placed them on shelves, in the cubby hole.

When being fitted out with shoes the girls would sit on the cold marble floor, outside the workroom door, waiting for Maggie to put in an appearance and unlock the cubby hole door, which could take some minutes. Taking advantage of the moment the girls would go into the boiler room and put their hands on the hot water pipes to warm up. Not often were we caught in the act of comfort, as we learned to discern the movement of footsteps within the workroom, which gave clear warning the door would spring open at any given time.

Often, Maggie would make you take a pair of shoes a bit too small or too large. If we were forced to wear a pair too small, we would make every effort to walk on the side of the shoe to try and break it down. With one hundred percent leather and expertise craftsmanship by St. Joseph's boys in repairing the shoes, this was difficult to do. If the leather didn't break down we would make every effort to destroy the strap across the shoe, hoping we could extract another pair from Maggie without getting into too much trouble. We achieved this destructive method by finding a large stone near the playing fields, and pounded it on the strap, until breaking the stitches loose.

Maggie knew all the tricks we were up to. One day when I presented my torn strap to her she promptly gave me a pair of shoes too big, with the result I ended up in the infirmary with bleeding blisters on my heels. I knew I was being punished for my sin, and that further atonement would present itself in the confessional box.

Sister Ethelreda, who looked after the health of the children, applied an ointment and plasters on the heels and told me to go back to the cubby hole for a smaller pair. When this scenario played out, Maggie growled, none too pleased.

Maggie eventually left St. Anne's and married an Irishman. They had two daughters. She continued living at Orpington, Kent, and took up local dress-making, at which she excelled. May Lyle, as guardian of the workroom, never held any one in doubt to the quality of her work and teaching, every stitch done to perfection.

Farmer Walsh lives on in our childhood memories, an endearing man.

As "children will be children," we often fell into some sort of mischief. Behind the playing fields were woods, and beyond them a farmer's apple orchards. Sometimes, when some of the older girls got into a rebellious mood, they would crawl under the barbed wire surrounding the fields and dash into the orchards to steal a few sour, green apples. The farmer would often hear the girls scrambling through the woods and breaking the branches off the trees so he would set his dogs on them. The barking of the dogs could be quite nerve-racking because one's concentration was to steal as many apples as possible. Some of the girls who got scared would run back to the playing field with no apples at all. If this embarrassing situation occurred, you could always expect to be called "Old Scary Cat" by the other girls.

Those who didn't scare easily from the dogs' barking, would tuck the apples up the legs of their knickers, hoping the elastic would 'hold out' and support the fruit. Then, every effort was made to run back the same way to the playing fields so as not to get caught for being out of bounds.

We often found it difficult, when bending down under the barbed wire, as the bulging of the apples caused them to keep popping out of the knicker legs and to roll all over the place. There was also risk of tearing one's clothing, hands and face, which alone pointed the accusing finger.

The culprits, if caught, knew the severity of punishment and expected it. In front of the whole school they were marched off to the Mother Superior's office and reprimanded with three strokes of the cane, on each hand. Tears and remorse fell in quick succession. To add fuel to the fire, the girls were then taken up to the infirmary and forced to drink a large dose of a foul liquid made from senna pods. This produced devastating effects on the intestinal system, and stomach pains raged for days. Only once did I try this foolish escapade for a dare. Caning I could almost endure – pods, no!

In July of each year we went for a two-weeks camping holiday at St. Mary's Bay, Dymchurch, a seaside resort in the County of Kent. We were packed into coaches, kit bag apiece, and holding additional clothing. Individual names and numbers were inked on tapes and sewn onto each bag – the owner being fully responsible for its contents. God help anyone who lost a garment! My number – 151 – was inked on shoes and clothing, and was also put above a tiny peg in the outside cloakroom where I hung my hat and coat. This system of numbering applied to all the girls, and often a younger girl, forgetting what number she was supposed to go by, would inadvertently take someone else's hat and coat. It was not unusual to see a small girl walk out of the cloakroom wearing a hat and coat two sizes too big for her.

Holidays were always a too-brief, happy time for the girls. Once seated and counted, and being hardly out of sight of the orphanage, we would start singing with lungs to bursting point – *'Ten Green Bottles Hanging on the Wall'* or *'Pack Up Your Troubles in Your Old Kit Bag and Smile'*, those were favourite songs. By the time this jolly crowd arrived safely at the holiday camp, the singing had reached a crescendo and could be heard for miles around. The local people always knew when the orphanage kids were coming.

Accommodation at the camp comprised forty camp beds per dormitory. Each girl was expected to keep her belongings and bed neat and tidy. Older girls assisted the younger ones. Toddlers and babies did not share this privilege and were left behind in the nursery at St. Anne's under the care of the staff.

Freedom of movement was more abundant in the mid–1930s at Dymchurch. Swimming or paddling in the sea, under the keen eyes of the nuns, and walking within certain boundaries of the camp, were permitted.

Occasionally, I would stop in my tracks to admire the surrounding countryside of this beautiful Kentish resort. The salty sea air invigorated one to the point of feeling utterly carefree, like a bird on the wing. To hear the wind rustling through the trees, sounding like a thousand tiny bells, the pounding of the rolling waves upon the sandy beach, alerted all my senses to the beauty of the landscape around me. Indeed, it was God's country, and only He could create such wonder.

If any girl was fortunate enough to possess a few pennies she could go off to the tiny tuck shop nearby in the village of Dymchurch and buy sherbet-dabs, liquorice ropes, gob-stoppers – which changed colours as you sucked them – or honeycomb bars; those were all my favourites.

The only way I was able to secure money was by scanning the fields and beaches. Finding the coins, I used to think how careless people were to waste money by losing it; nevertheless, when discovering the treasure,

I was elated. Wherever I walked, my eyes never left the ground, and never a day passed when I didn't pick up either a sixpence or a penny.

As I grew older I began to appreciate the power of a penny and what luxuries it bought, either by way of a new friend or in the form of a tasty treat. Life was becoming sweeter for me in more ways than one. I developed an awareness of my peers and quickly judged their behavioural patterns, responding to them accordingly to the benefit of my own existence. Orphanage life was, without fully comprehending, an exercise in the art of survival.

From the age of twelve – two years prior to becoming an "old girl" at the age of fourteen – weekly cookery and home economics classes were taken by the girls. In the 1920s these classes were originally held next to the dark boiler room on the lower floor, beneath the long, marble corridor. To get to it the girls walked along the long, marble corridor, turned right at the top of it, then proceeded to go up six wide, concrete steps to reach a landing. To the right of the landing there was a large kitchen; to the left, a narrow, short staircase which led down to the boiler-room, cookery classroom and storeroom. These areas were dark and always smelled extremely musty – perhaps due to lack of windows and fresh air.

Having seen rats and mice running around the boiler-room, we were frightened to go near for fear they would attack us. Everywhere could be seen the tell-tale signs of chewed-up bars of soap in the storeroom and droppings round the large wooden chests holding flour, tea and sugar.

By the time I attended these classes, in the late '30s, they were held in an upper room leading from the long, marble corridor, which gave us more light and air in which to learn the skills of cookery and home economics.

Mrs. Walker was our teacher. She was as tall as stout, with light, brown hair. Most noticeable about her were her enormous red hands, such as those an Irish navvy would be proud of. She lived outside the orphanage, and took cookery and home economic classes twice a week. She was well-liked, and kind when speaking to the girls. A non-Catholic, we all thought she was great! When saying prayers before and after class we noticed with some amusement her hands seemed to be confused as to which way she should make the sign of the cross, but we tried not to giggle. Her on-going philosophy in home economics was that, when sweeping a room the corners needed special attention, while the centre of the room "took care of itself."

At exam time those with top marks were given a prize everyone was anxious to achieve, knowing at the end of it we would be given, as a reward, one of her old handbags.

During one particular cookery lesson, Mrs. Walker was to teach us how to make "jam puffs." Wearing long white aprons over our gym tunics, we all stood round the long table where she proceeded to show us how to mix flour and fat into crumbs, then bind it together with cold water, before rolling the pastry out onto a floured board. This done, we then cut the pastry into small squares and onto each one placed a spoonful of jam, then folded the edges of the pastry to seal in the jam. The puffs were then placed on a tin tray and put into the oven to bake.

Twenty minutes later they were ready to come out of the oven. It was at this stage that my friend Pat decided to reach out and quickly whip one of the puffs from the tray and tuck it up underneath one of the legs of her knickers.

Simultaneously, the door leading from the outside corridor suddenly swung open! Looking through the cookery class window, Sister Kevin caught my friend red-handed in the act of stealing. The timing couldn't have been more perfect. Without further ado, and without the courtesy of asking Mrs. Walker for permission to enter her class, Sister Kevin threw open the classroom door and, like a raging bull, stormed over to my friend and walloped her in the exact spot where she had hidden the jam puff.

Screaming at her, she yelled, 'How dare you steal, you wicked, sinful girl! You will burn in purgatory!'

Although Pat was determined not to cry, the moment Sister Kevin left the classroom, without a word spoken to Mrs. Walker, my friend let out a blood-curdling scream as the hot jam was now unmercifully running down her leg at an alarming speed, causing her to hop madly from one leg to the other.

While these theatrics were being played out, the class stood back in shocked silence. Mrs. Walker stood like a statue, with her huge red hands raised high above her head, as though in prayer, her mouth wide open.

Shortly after the class regained its composure, Mrs. Walker cut some of the puffs into small squares and handed a piece to each girl. Needless to say, Pat was not included in this special treat.

On another occasion Pat, Madeline and I were doing odd jobs in the kitchen when the nun-in-charge told Pat to refill a tin container from the flour bin, as the nun needed this for making some pastry.

Upon entering the kitchen, to the left side of the wall stood three large wooden bins, with heavy wooden lids. One held tea, the other sugar and the third, white flour. These bins were filled up from supplies taken from the storeroom, next to the boiler-room.

With the tin container in one hand, Pat opened the wooden lid of the flour bin and leaned in. As she tried to scoop flour into the container with a small shovel in her other hand, this petite slim girl suddenly found herself slipping deeper and deeper into the flour bin, her legs thrashing the air wildly in an attempt to stop herself from falling.

Watching this performance and seeing Pat's elastic navy blue bloomers in full view, we two began to go into fits of laughter. Although we couldn't speak for giggling we were a bit concerned as to how we could get her out of the bin before the kitchen nun spotted her or heard Pat's muffled pleas for help.

Suddenly Sister Attracta, the Head Mistress, came into the kitchen demanding to know what all the commotion was about.

With considerable effort between the two of us, we hoisted Pat by her legs out the wooden bin. Sister was not amused, neither was Pat, who was covered from head to waist in flour, having left the empty tin container in the bottom of the bin. She looked a mess. She had no face. Not given to crying, even if Pat wanted to, she couldn't, as the flour was stuck firmly to her eyes.

The kitchen nun had busied herself with other work while waiting for Pat to give her the tin container, oblivious to the goings on. She was suddenly aware of the Head Mistress in the kitchen. She ordered us to clean-up Pat but before doing so, to find John Bannon, a strapping hulk of a good-looking Irishman, who looked after the boiler-room and did general maintenance around the orphanage. Having found him within the perimeter of the school we walked with him as far as the kitchen area but didn't wait to see how he would react to the two nuns waiting for him, with an order to retrieve the tin flour container down at the very bottom of the bin.

We then set-to with a small hand brush, used for cleaning crumbs off the refectory tables, and a cloth from the scullery, to remove most of the flour from Pat's head, face and clothing. How she would explain the reason to May Lyle in the workroom for a need to change her clothing, we left that entirely to her. That done, the two of us scampered off to the playground, laughing.

Pat, who with her sister Kathleen came over from Ireland at an early age, was a stunningly beautiful Irish girl, with soft pale blue eyes and black curly hair. Be it her nature or not, or perhaps driven by some unknown fear, she displayed an unruly attitude and boldness against authority that continually landed her into trouble; she took risks most of the girls wouldn't dream of, without fear of being caught. But I secretly admired her. She had determination and courage of spirit that would not be broken. I often wondered if it was her beauty that so riled a certain nun who punished her, repeatedly, for no apparent reason.

With all the cakes, scones and pastries the girls made at class, we often wondered on whose table they would eventually land; it certainly was not the refectory where we ate.

Having reached twelve years, two or three girls were allowed, by Sister Kevin, to slice bread. The bread room was about six by seven feet long. It had wooden shelves on the walls and wooden countertop, on which stood a bread-cutting machine. Before my time in the bread room, the machine was operated by a wooden handle which caused awful pains to the muscles if used too long. The bread room was always a favourite place of the girls; it was like being in a snug, warm sanctuary where they could work without anyone looking over them. As the bread room adjoined the kitchen, it was never cold.

St. Joseph's baked all the buns and bread for St. Anne's. The boys would deliver the warm, square loaves on large wooden trays, through the tradesmen's entrance, leading to the bread room. Boys seen in our midst, other than at church services, were a rarity – so as we grew older many of us would ogle-eye at them and choose secretly the one you hoped, one day, would be your boyfriend.

Not only did St. Joseph's supply us with bread, but also vegetables, which were grown on their small farm. And, occasionally, we would be treated to a basketful of small, red eating apples, picked off their trees.

During the hot summer days of August, a group of us girls would sit on the grass in the playing field, in a large circle, and the nun-in-charge would pass round a tin bucket loaded with left-off lettuce leaves, which came from the farm. Each girl would take a handful of lettuce and, like rabbits, would chew and chew until the bucket was emptied. We must have looked a happy sight!

It was a mid-week day when my friends Pat, Theresa and I were delegated "slicing and spreading" in the bread room. The cutting machine with its wooden handle had now been replaced by an electric machine, which took a flip of a switch for the machine to operate. One girl would put a loaf into the machine, the other would take the slices off and pile them high onto large wooden trays, ready for "spreading". I usually ended up with this job, using margarine or dripping, which was sparsely spread on each slice of bread.

As we happily jogged along with our tasks, crispy, warm crumbs were gently falling at a continuous pace from the vibrating bread machine. So they wouldn't be wasted or fall onto the floor, we'd scooped them up with our hands and put them into neat little piles on top of the countertop. Eventually, crumbs were everywhere, so after finishing slicing and spreading the bread we put clean cloths over each tray, ready to be served at the next meal.

Thinking we had the right to help ourselves, each of us with tiny hands took piles of crumbs and stuffed them hungrily into our mouths. The joy of this treat knew no bounds!

Happily chewing on the crumbs, without the slightest thought in our heads we could be stealing, we didn't hear the bread room door open and for several seconds were unaware that Sister Kevin was standing there watching three guilty little workers with hands and faces covered in bread crumbs.

'Hurry up, girls,' she cried. 'Sweep up the floor, before the tea bell rings.'

Doing as we were bid, we brushed the crumbs off our hands and faces, swept the countertop and floor, laughing heartily on the way out for being caught "in the act".

Throughout my growing-up years at St. Anne's I often noticed that when the girls were sent on errands by the nuns, they always carried with them large tins. This contingency of "shoppers" made me wonder why there was always so much activity going on with girls scurrying here, there and everywhere, at a lively pace. As most of them were older than me, I was smart enough to know that asking questions could be risky, so I would just stare at this on-going performance and hope one day I'd discover the reason for all the activity. All too soon, I was to find out!

Caught one day by Sister Vincent, a nun of enormous proportions in charge of the dormitories, she handed me a large empty tin and ordered me to go to the store room, fill it up with Cardinal red polish and bring it back to the infants' dormitories. Executing the nun's order as fast as I could run, I dashed up a flight of stairs leading from the long, marble corridor and headed for the dormitories, with the tin wobbling in my hand. Upon arriving, I was somewhat surprised to see Theresa, with whom I'd spent time in the bread room, standing there next to the nun.

Sister's instructions were that the two dormitories, separated by the nun's cubicle and lavatory, needed to be waxed and polished. She handed Theresa the heavy tin of wax, in which stood a wooden spatula. I was told to get a black rubber kneeling pad and old pieces of rags and bits of blanket from under the cupboard near the lavatory, which I did. Sister then promptly disappeared, leaving us to it.

Theresa began working from the top end of the dormitory and carried on into the other dormitory, by dipping the spatula into the tin and throwing dollops of wax onto the floor, sometimes narrowly missing my head by inches.

My job was to kneel on the rubber pad and, with a piece of rag, rub the dollops into the linoleum until it was all rubbed in. This done,

Theresa and I took some string and with it tied pieces of blanket over the soles of our shoes and "skated" along both dormitories, stopping only a couple of times to replace the old piece of blanket – now showing remarkable signs of heavy paraffin red wax, with a cleaner piece – then continuing up and down, to give the floor a glasslike polish.

We were both heading for the final lap, pleased and smiling at our results, when we decided to charge down the dormitories for one last time. I went first, and finished my lap. Theresa, her arms outstretched, took a huge breath and with all the energy she could muster, charged from the top of one dormitory to the next with such intensity that in so doing, landed smack into Sister Vincent who had entered by the dormitory door and from the impact was almost thrown off her feet.

Sister's face was red.

'Sorry, Sister,' we spluttered. 'We didn't mean to hurt you.'

We dared not to touch or help straighten her crumpled, sacred clothing.

Hearing her give a weak grunt, we held our breath as we watched Sister gingerly step over the polished floor, hoping she wouldn't slip up, as she disappeared safely into her tiny cubicle.

Gathering up the cleaning rags and empty tin that we threw back into the cupboard, with careless rapture, the two of us then fled down to the playground, laughing our heads off!

Everything we did at St. Anne's was done in a mechanical style and if a job, like bed-making, wasn't carried out to the satisfaction of the nun-in-charge, she would begin her endless preaching about being sinful for getting into bad habits. In a method that caused much consternation to many girls, she would then show them how all bedding should be "enveloped" at each corner of the mattress, so it wasn't left hanging over the side; a task most of us found heavy and, we thought, unnecessary. However, we kept this opinion strictly to ourselves, to avoid punishment. Strange as it may seem, to this day, I continue bed-making "envelopes".

Rigid rules were observed at all times and one dared not stray far from them, for fear of committing a mortal sin. This instilled in us an inferiority complex, which prevailed throughout our childhood, causing emotional stress and anxiety. Despite a girl's best effort to do a job right when undertaking a task however small, it was never considered good enough. That we might develop into normal adult human beings would, I felt, be a test of our ability to survive.

By the time I reached fourteen years I had finished with classroom curriculum and, as with the other girls of the same age, I was expected to work round the orphanage for the next two years, as an unpaid servant. The idea of being paid wages was preposterous.

The duties we had to perform included doing the laundry, tidying the kitchen, and helping to prepare vegetables. Also, sweeping the floors in the refectory, polishing the dormitories, and cleaning staircases. We also repaired the children's clothes in the workroom, as well as cleaned the nuns' sitting and dining rooms. Mother Superior would leave you in a job which suited you, or that you enjoyed doing. There was one job, however, I had to do many times which I must confess I resented doing, that being the scrubbing of the large refectory – all of a hundred feet long.

Every Friday evening, after the last meal of the day which consisted of bread and dripping and cocoa, four of us girls would gather in the refectory and with our gym tunics tucked inside our blue knickers, we would each take on a quarter section of the floor area. Kneeling on rubber pads, and using large buckets filled to the brim with hot soda water and scrubbing brushes, we scrubbed back to back until meeting each other in the centre of the floor. Then, turning around, we faced each other, and so as not to leave any dirty rings or tidemarks, we scrubbed the centre of the floor as hard as possible until clean.

The refectory floor was always the blackest and grittiest of all the areas in the orphanage as it was used three times daily during meal-times by hundreds of tiny tramping feet. The work took the best part of three hours and when we had finished the cleaning, the four of us would stand back proudly admiring the good, clean job we had done. We emptied the filthy water down the drain in the scullery, and then scrubbed our hands, arms and knees with large blocks of yellow soap, hoping all the dirty, slimy watermarks would come off. Our treat before retiring to bed was another mug of hot cocoa and a "doorstep" of bread and marg.

Another duty included answering the front door. I remember clearly one particular sunny, Sunday afternoon, when the doorbell rang. I sprinted down the long, marble corridor cautiously glancing over my shoulder to see if I would be caught, by a nun, in the act of running instead of walking. I opened the big, oak door to a gentleman, named Mr. Hall, who had called to see his two daughters. I led him into the vestibule, through to a door on the left, and into a tiny, cold marble-floored cubicle, comprising two wooden chairs. Adjoining the cubicle was a lavatory. Indicating to one of the wooden chairs in the dismal cubicle, I asked Mr. Hall to 'please sit down while I fetch your daughters.'

The vestibule area had another door leading from it to the right which was called "The Reception Room." In comparison, this room was well-furnished, pleasantly warm and comfortable; it was reserved, however, for "special occasions" of visiting bishops, priests and other official dignitaries, who were served tea or luncheon from the best silverware.

Having reported the visitor to the nun in the office, I ran off to the playground, spotted the two Hall girls and took them back to the cubicle to visit with their father. I liked Mr. Hall. He was tall and slim, with black hair, and he always spoke kindly to me when I opened the front door to him. This Sunday, smiling, he handed me a large red apple, which I humbly, but much embarrassed, accepted. Never had I seen an apple like this one before!

Dashing back, again checking to see if I would be caught running, I went out of the door at the top end of the corridor and turned right toward the playground. Leaping up the concrete steps two at a time and oblivious to all, I began devouring this luscious treat, gouging great teeth marks into the core of the apple; the delicious juice ran all over my mouth.

Suddenly, without any warning, a voice bellowed, 'Where did you get that from?'

Turning swiftly around, I came face to face with the head school teacher, Sister Attracta. Although a tiny nun, who always threw her black veil over her shoulder when she got angry, her voice could override that of any sergeant major. She had a habit of lolling her head from side to side, giving the impression it would fall off at any given time during her screaming session.

Her long, black holy clothing engulfed her tiny frame and fell into thick folds from the weight of the cloth. Round her small waist was a thick strap and rosary beads, which were used in sharp contrast; one to punish and the other with which to pray. The sting of the strap, whipped across my legs one day because I was caught laughing in the classroom, is an experience I have never forgotten.

Sister's face was stormy. Almost choking with fright, and petrified a wallop might be in the offing, I meekly whispered, 'Mr. Hall gave it to me.'

'Be off with you, girl,' she said gruffly.

I didn't have the heart to finish off the apple; my appetite gone, I tossed away the remains of it.

Worried of having committed a mortal sin, and feeling the need to repent for my greed, I went into the playground. There I plonked myself down on the long, cold hard bench and pounding my chest, whispering, 'Mea culpa, mea culpa,' and asked God for his forgiveness.

Since I was now one of the older girls, Mother Marcellena, in whose presence I felt most comfortable, showed her trust and confidence in me by sending me on small errands beyond the boundaries of the orphanage. Sometimes, it would be a visit to a small chemist shop in Orpington high street, or to pick up a prescription from the local doctor's house. On other occasions I would take a parishioner's little girl, who attended catechism in the church on Saturdays, to the bus stop, and board her safely. For these tasks "Mother" would compensate me with a coin or two, depending on the size of the task delegated. I always had to report back to her, in her small office, the minute I returned "home".

Clutching the pennies, farthings or halfpennies, I would take the money and tuck it into a little bag which I had made from old rag taken from the workroom, tie a knot in it and hide it safely under the mattress of my bed. I did this when I thought it was safe to do so, without the spying eyes of the nuns or girls. Faithfully, whenever earning more money I added it secretly to the rag bag, which always seemed to weigh heavy but, in fact, never held more than sixpence.

I was beginning to accumulate a nice little nest-egg and felt extremely important and pleased with myself until one day, reaching beneath the mattress for the rag bag, I discovered to my horror that it wasn't there! I searched frantically for the rag bag, checking under the full length of the mattress; alas, it was nowhere to be found. Obviously, I'd been caught in the act of hiding my treasure, and someone had stolen it!

I told God, 'You will have to find the thief for me,' but He never revealed her identity.

Undaunted, and having further earnings of farthings and pennies, I made another rag bag. However, this time I was determined, somehow, to keep it safely on my person, which was no easy task, when one was made to strip and wash in front of nuns and girls. In due course when the money accumulated to sixpence, I asked Mother Marcellena for permission to spend it in Mr. Freeman's tiny tuck shop, situated just outside the boundaries of the orphanage. You could buy all sorts of goodies with a farthing – rock candy, pear drops, dolly mixtures and the like – and I came "home" with plenty of treats which I shared among my school friends.

During my "in-house training" period, May Lyle entrusted me with the cleaning of her shoes – a job I enjoyed doing. Each week, four or five pairs of shoes would be lined up outside her bedroom door. Going along to her small room on the upper floor above the long, marble corridor, I picked up the shoes and took them into the workroom where May Lyle kept the cleaning materials. According to their colour, black or cream polish was liberally applied to the shoes and I polished them until they shone like beacons.

A tiny brush, with soft rubber spikes on it, was used to gently smooth over the uppers of the suede shoes to bring up the pile. When the job was finished May Lyle would inspect the shoes very carefully and once satisfied, she would say, 'Take the shoes and put them back outside my bedroom door.'

Before leaving the workroom, she would take my hand and press into it a threepenny piece. The first time this happened I was so elated, I could have hugged her; however, such a display of emotion would never have been allowed, and could be misinterpreted as greed. What wealth! No farthings ever came forth from May Lyle.

In 1938, I would see my last summer holiday at Dymchurch. With the outbreak of war in 1939 the camp closed, and the lovely sandy beaches were heavily barricaded with coils of barbed wire. We all wondered what would happen to the fairground which gave us so much fun, and the "dolly train" that chugged right alongside the chalets and caravans on the sea front. I thought of the long summer evenings, when a number of us children would sit on the long concrete wall facing out to sea and watch, fascinated, the delightful romping and rolling of the black porpoises swimming close to the shore. The warm red sun lit up the reeds that grew on the marshes, and would cast a magnificent glow around the sheep in the fields. We called it "shepherd's delight".

Everyone, including the nuns, would miss Dymchurch. Memories linger of the mounds of food we devoured there in the large canteen. Breakfasts of large bowls of steaming porridge, plates of delicious, fat beef sausages with tinned tomatoes, mountains of bread and margarine, and all the milk you could drink. Dinner meals of hot stews, meat and vegetables, fish and meat pies were followed by scrumptious desserts. Tea-time provided lots of bread and jam and huge slices of cake. The crowning glory of the day was more slices of delicious Naffy cake – either plain or made with caraway seeds – and a hot mug of cocoa.

The holidays over, we returned to the reality of life at the orphanage looking the picture of health with tans and, of course, all packing a few more pounds of weight. Dymchurch days were fun days, never to be forgotten. We were lucky, indeed, specially during such impoverished times of the 1930s to be given the opportunity of exploring this beautiful Kentish resort, all due to the generosity of a daily newspaper in London, England, who financed the holidays for the children of St. Anne's, as well as other orphanage children.

This wonderful, carefree, feeling of freedom unknown to the girls before, saw them "throw caution to the wind", and take advantage of any situation that appealed to them. Sometimes including the nuns, we stayed outside the boundaries of the camp for a longer-than-allowed period. I was a prime culprit for doing this, as I wandered aimlessly along the shoreline with thoughts of my own, while breathing in the salty sea air; the wind caressing my hair. It was an exhilarating time for me and one I would never forget. Most of us hoped, in our hearts, these jolly times at Dymchurch would never end.

With the news of the war, one sensed the apprehension of what was to come, and how the pattern of our lifestyle would dramatically change. The ground floor in the main building of the orphanage was turned into dormitories and if the bombing was bad during the day or night-time, nuns, staff and children crowded into the crypt under the Holy Innocents church.

Caroline "Carrie" Marshall at age 16,
sent out "into the world" in 1941.

School lessons were disrupted by sirens that caused chaos despite repeated drills of where the girls were to go in the event a bombing raid got under way. Mother Marcellena's main concern was always for the safety of the children, making sure like a mother hen caring for her brood of chicks, that they were all tucked away in the sanctuary of God's crypt.

Orpington, being very close to Biggin Hill airport – a prime enemy target – was incessantly raided. After the bombings we would find pieces of shrapnel around the school yard and playing fields but we were not, of course, allowed to keep the shrapnel or anything else we were likely to find.

One particular morning, after a noisy raid on the airport the previous night, we came out of the church crypt to find the infirmary had received a direct hit and was flattened to the ground. Debris was everywhere. This set some of the nuns off into a panic as they scurried to see if any other part of the orphanage had been damaged.

Strangely enough, as the nuns put it, 'it was the will of God that only the infirmary was bombed.' The church, hardly a few yards away from the infirmary, didn't have one damaged brick.

We often watched from the playground many aeroplanes spiralling the skies, thundering and roaring off to some foreign land or unknown battle with the enemy. We prayed daily for the young, brave pilots and hoped the war would soon be over so they could, one day, return safely home.

In 1941, Mr. R.A. Butler, then known as 'Rab' Butler became Minister of Education and responsible for *The Education Act*. Educational systems began to change. This news was not well received by the headmistress of St. Anne's, who thought Mr. Butler an interfering busybody, but wouldn't say so to his face.

Changes to the girls' education were made according to the *Act*, regardless of whether the nuns liked it or not. *The Education Act* opened the door for many St. Anne's girls who had high grades and allowed them to take their exams for entry into Grammar or Commercial schools. The days of being pushed into domestic service to work in Catholic homes, without any thought of assessing a girl's intelligence first, thank God, were seemingly over.

Rapid changes took place, and St. Anne's Orphanage became known as St. Anne's School, gradually opening its classroom doors to other Catholic children living in the area. Instead of being communally institutionalized, the girls were housed in small family units, built within the compound of the school and were supervised by one nun who was fully responsible for her charges. I was extremely pleased with this turn of event, which was long past due, and happy for those girls at St. Anne's who were now going to be brought up in a better environment. At the same time, I felt sad that these opportunities had not availed themselves to me and my friends when we were at school.

In 1941, at the age of sixteen, I was discharged from St. Anne's. May Lyle sent word for me to report to the workroom and discard my school clothes. My "going away" outfit included a long, brown wool coat with a "Robin Hood" style hat – feather and all, thick lyle stockings and brown laced-up shoes.

May Lyle took a last look at me and wished me 'Goodbye,' adding, 'Work hard, Carrie, and you'll get on well.'

It was the only time I could remember her calling me by my name.

Leaving by the workroom door, I stepped inside the adjoining room which was the Reception Room, and took a good look around, thinking, decidedly, how warm and comfortable it was. There was no comparison between the Reception Room and the tiny cubicle used for visiting parents, which was always so cold and uninviting.

I went through to the vestibule area at the front door where several of the "old girls" were waiting to see me off. All "puffed out", Mother Marcellena finally arrived on the scene with a staff member. She looked approvingly at my outfit and said she hoped I would do well in my job.

Kissing me goodbye and thrusting a shilling piece in my hand, she said, 'Keep up your religion, my child,' and disappeared behind the big, front oak door, her habit literally "flying".

Walking down the avenue with the staff member, I tearfully looked back at the bare, front windows of the dormitories to catch sight of several of the girls waving their goodbyes – a recognized ritual when a girl left school. I knew I would miss them. Over the years I had developed a close relationship with many of the girls in my own age group, with whom I had attended classes. We always stuck up for one another when a girl was beaten by nun or staff. The consoling was very real; the loyalty profound.

OUT INTO THE WORLD

It never dawned on me until I went, as the nuns put it, "out into the world", how vastly different was my upbringing compared to that of a child who lived with his or her own parents. This feeling of being "different" from other people had disastrous effects on me in that I lacked confidence in myself. I lived in constant fear that some inquisitive mind would discover my background and the stigma of my upbringing. Like shadows creeping in every corner, I feared images from the past would suddenly spring out and reveal themselves. As I was soon to learn, life in the "outside world" was tough – there was no choice between the two evils.

The staff member and I reached Orpington railway station in time to catch the one o'clock train to London. Upon arriving at Charing Cross station, I was then transferred onto another train going southbound to East Grinstead in the County of Sussex, and was instructed by the staff member to get off the train when it reached its destination. She told me I would be met at the station by a lady, whose name she failed to tell me.

The train, crowded with soldiers carrying full packs, had no available seats and a young soldier offered me his, which I accepted. Towering above me, he started up a conversation but being so naïve, I had no idea what he was talking about. I merely sat, mute, and listened to him for most of the journey. I'm sure he must have thought, 'what a strange kid.'

Arriving at East Grinstead station I stepped down onto the platform and a middle-aged, stout, grey-haired lady approached me, inquiring: 'Is that you, Miss Marshall?'

She introduced herself to me as Miss Finnigan, assistant cook. Picking up my utility suitcase, we left the railway station and walked, in silence, down the long narrow country lane lined with hawthorn hedges. Friesian cows were pasturing in a nearby field – a sight I had never seen at close quarters before – so I paused to get a closer look at them.

While we were passing the farmer's gate, some of the cows went on chewing, while others simply stood glaring at us with their sad, mournful eyes. I felt an urge to run and thrust open the gate and set the cows free, but the sound of Miss Finnigan's clopping shoes was like a formidable warning, telling me not to interfere with these creatures confined behind barbed wire.

Having walked well beyond three miles, we finally arrived at a large red brick building and passed through tall iron-spiked gates. Unbeknown to me at the time this was a reformatory home for boys, called St. Thomas Moore, where I was to work as a house parlour maid for a weekly wage of five shillings.

Entering the building, a wave of despair swept over me. I couldn't grasp why I had been sent to this outlandish place which was miles from anywhere. From the time of leaving the station, I had passed not but one soul.

'Another prison,' I thought to myself. 'Would there be no escaping?'

Little did I realize that within a matter of months I would be doing just that, as I felt I had no choice but to get away from this dreadful place.

The assistant cook escorted me to an office where I was introduced to the Matron. An Irish lady of mid-years, she was petite, well-groomed, and her face had a lovely soft, pink glow. She offered me a chair and asked me several questions, to which I replied with either a 'yes' or 'no'.

'You can start your duties in the morning,' she said. 'Dorothy, the kitchen help, will show you what to do.'

The interview was over.

Introductions were made to the rest of the kitchen staff by Miss Finnigan, who then led me upstairs to the attic and showed me into a tiny bedroom.

'Come down to the staff room when you're ready,' said Miss Finnigan, 'and have some tea.'

Leaving me to unpack my few belongings, she retired back downstairs.

I looked around the room whose furnishings consisted of a single wrought-iron bedstead, a chest of drawers and a chair. Slowly, a wave of apprehension swept over me. I wanted to cry. For the first time in my life I was completely alone. I felt scared, and already missed the company of the girls at the orphanage. I went over to a small bedroom window and looked down below at well-kept lawns and colourful flower beds. The fields beyond were of lush green, and farther over, more cows were pasturing in the meadow.

St. Thomas Moore was run by the Christian Brothers. Attending religious services and practicing the teachings of Catholicism were much the same there, as at St. Anne's. The hierarchy never failed to instruct me as to which of the masses, benedictions or confessions I was to attend; this routine of services never altered.

My stay at East Grinstead was a short one. The only thing I liked about the place was the surrounding countryside, which sharpened my senses to its beauty and gave me a feeling of utter peace. I could spend hours listening to the birds; the ever-whispering of the wind in the trees was magic to the soul.

Money being scarce, and also the nearest town of Horsham being too far away, I spent my half-days off work wandering in a nearby meadow, cautiously on the look-out for farmer, bull or cows.

Finding a secluded spot, hidden from view, I would sit down on the soft meadow grass and count the different species of birds. Fascinated, I watched as they hopped and flew from tree to tree, unaware of my presence, and listened to their calls and songs. If I sat very still several rabbits would come sniffing nervously close by; hares and pheasants also appearing. My idle, tranquil hours were enjoyably spent, in total oblivion to life's demands, watching nature's delightful creatures' strange, uninhibited performances. Although alone in the meadow I never felt lonely; contentment and peace of mind folded over me like a soft, warm blanket.

I detested the work at the reformatory and was constantly worried of being behind schedule with my duties, which were heavy and dirty. Prior to serving breakfast to the Brothers, another duty was to clean their sitting-room and, upon entering, I would gasp for breath due to the after-effects of heavy tobacco smoking, from the night before.

I was always in a dreadful state of nervousness, causing me to drop and break things. One of the Brothers, short and slimly built, with brown, curly hair, had the most piercing blue eyes I've ever seen and that petrified me. His constant gaze followed my movements everywhere and made me feel most uncomfortable. I could not comprehend this interest in me, yet knew he intended no good. One of my duties included cleaning his bedroom and I would dash in and out, barely flicking at the dust on the furniture, which resulted in strong complaints being made to the Matron. I was terrified he would trap me in his bedroom. Although sloppiness was foreign to my nature I could not give Matron the reason for it, as I felt that whatever explanation I gave her, she would not have believed me.

One day, an opportunity to escape from the reformatory availed itself to me when I was accused, by the Matron, of a misdemeanour, causing me to become so upset that the accusing finger should have been pointed at me.

With brazen nerve and courage, and without thinking of the consequences of my action, I gathered up my meagre possessions and pride – and ran away. Running as fast as I could to the nearest bus stop, I boarded a Green-line bus to Horsham, and from there caught another bus going to Hove, and headed to Canon Crea's house situated on Norton Road.

Canon Crea was one of the Trustees of the Southwark Catholic Children's Rescue Society, who commuted between Sussex, Kent and London. A happy-go-lucky man, he visited St. Anne's a few times a year and the girls absolutely adored him. Not very tall, a little on the rotund side, he had light, sandy-colour, fine hair. Of ruddy complexion, he wore a smile from ear to ear. The affection the girls had for him was, without

Canon Crea, a trustee of the
Catholic Children's Rescue Society.

doubt, reciprocated by him in a genuine, caring manner. His interest was in all the children and to each one, his affection abounded.

On one of his visits to the orphanage, as he stepped down onto the concrete steps in the playground accompanied by Mother Superior, the girls, "throwing caution to the wind", hugged and clung on to him tightly. His face beaming, Mother Superior unsuccessfully tried to extricate him from what seemed like the thousand arms of an octopus. I was about thirteen years old at the time, and standing a few yards away from this merry throng, when the Canon noticed my distance and, with a finger, beckoned me toward him.

Shyly approaching him, he asked what had happened to cause such red finger marks and swelling across my right eye. 'Come,' he persisted. 'Tell me.'

As the chatter of the girls ceased, there was a deadly hush. Feeling all eyes upon me, I proceeded to explain to the Canon that a nun had ordered me to go down to the storeroom in the cellar and bring back a large block of yellow soap.

'Hurry, girl!' the nun had called after me.

Executing an order of such urgency it was a question of whether to hop, skip, jump or run – I chose the latter, cautiously aware it was strictly forbidden within the walls of the orphanage.

Upon reaching the storeroom, which held household cleaning materials, there were other girls waiting to be served by the staff member in charge. Noting the situation and realizing that Sister's patience would wear thin if the soap was not brought to her immediately, I saw where the soap was kept on the floor and automatically bent down to pick up a slab. As I was about to get up, a staff member, Mary Donahue, gave me a backhander across the face which stung me so much that for a minute I wondered what had hit me.

The Canon listened quietly and then saying 'goodbye' to the girls, left the playground with Mother Superior walking close behind. What transpired between them is anyone's guess, but never again did that staff member, or anyone else, hit me.

Mary Donahue, along with her sisters Kathleen and Eileen, came from Ireland. All were brought up at St. Anne's from an early age. When reaching sixteen, Mary stayed on to work as a staff member, while her two sisters were sent out to work as domestic servants. As I was to evaluate later in my growing-up years, of the three sisters, Eileen appeared the most likeable and gentle. Kathleen, the eldest, only visited St. Anne's occasionally so I wasn't able to judge her fully, although whenever I saw her she always looked stern. Mary, on the other hand, had an outgoing personality with a yen for the opposite sex, be it priest, bishop, or the Christian Brothers. She was tall and slim, and accentuated her bosom to the full, by wearing low-cut blouses. Often as kids we would sneak a peek, to see why she chose to expose her flesh. Her strong character, and why she badly treated the girls the way she did, left me perplexed, in view of the fact that her upbringing was on the same strict principles as the rest of us. I thought that because of this, she might have shown a little more compassion or pity when reprimanding a child, but she never did. Her punishments were as harsh as the nuns. Deep down, she may have thought that if she showed any sign of weakness in front of the nuns, they might assume a child was getting off lightly. That was not, however, how the system worked.

Mary Donahue and Sister Kevin were in charge of the refectory. From large, steel serving pots they would ladle out the food to each child holding a dinner plate below the lip of the serving pot. If for some obscure reason Mary felt you didn't deserve the food she would crash the ladle down onto the plate, causing it to break in two pieces, splattering the food all over the countertop. The unfortunate girl would be made to clean up the mess, and go hungry. The rest of the girls waiting to be served, were shocked in silence. This episode was repeated time and time again.

'Suffer little children, come unto me,' said the Lord. To suffer the stigma of birth was one thing, but to be constantly humiliated throughout childhood was another agony of sin we all endured at St. Anne's.

In her late thirties, Mary married the brother of one of the ladies who sang in the church choir. They had two children. The last time I saw her was on the sands at Dymchurch, in the late 1950s. We passed each other, without a word spoken.

Visiting Orpington in 1984, I found that St. Anne's, St. Joseph's and the Holy Innocents church had been demolished, and that the land bought many years ago by the Southwark Diocese was sold to developers for a private housing estate. No doubt, part of the deal to the developers was for them to build a small convent house for the remaining elderly nuns. I must confess this turn of event pleased me, as I realized that here anyway, child abuse had slipped beneath the rubble, never to surface.

Calling at the convent house, I was invited in by one of the nuns whom I knew from the "old days". Upon entering, I recognized several statues that had been taken from the Holy Innocents church, standing in the hallway. We visited the chapel, and then I was led into the nuns' sitting-room, where I noticed a nun strapped in a high-backed chair.

'Look who's come to see you, Kevin? It's Carrie,' said the escorting nun.

There was no response. Peering closer at this fragile figure, I slowly recognized the face of Sister Kevin. She had had a severe stroke. Of all the nuns at St. Anne's, Sister Kevin had to be the most feared. Whenever I saw her approaching I would run and hide behind one of the lavatory doors in the playground, until I felt it safe to come out. If I could avoid seeing her at all cost I would do so, to escape the full wrath of her tongue that could cut into you like a knife slicing butter. Forever fearful of doing something wrong I would scurry along, like a frightened mouse, disappearing into a hole.

I remember her as being tall in stature, with steely blue eyes, and an aquiline nose. Her teeth that once protruded over her lower lip had now been replaced with dentures. We used to call her "Buckteeth". No longer purposeful of stride, her white hair cut short at the ears, and her piercing blue eyes, once capable of penetrating one's soul, simply gazed into space. I looked at this once domineering nun who used to frighten the daylights out of the girls and, sadly, could not in all sincerity find it in my heart to feel any sympathy for her.

While everyone attending the 1894-1994 Centenary of the Sisters of Mercy in Orpington recognized that Sister Kevin had indeed been a hard-working nun and spent most of her religious life in the service of God, I cannot, however, accept that she gave any joyous service to the young children during my time at St. Anne's.

When I arrived at Canon Crea's house, I rang the doorbell which was answered by Madeline, one of my dearest school friends. When our eyes met, the look of surprise was of disbelief, and her first words uttered were: 'Gosh, what are you doing here, then?'

Briefly, I explained I had run away from my job.

'Oh, you'd better come in,' said Madeline, 'but God only knows what the Canon will have to say.'

When Canon Crea returned to his house, he requested I see him in his study. His conversation with me was one of kindness and understanding after I explained to him how unhappy I had been at East Grinstead. I didn't of course go into detail about the Brother who had terrorized me with his on-going gaze, as I found the subject too embarrassing. On leaving his study he told me I could stay in his household for a few days and share some of the duties with his staff, who were mainly girls I knew from St. Anne's. I was happy to do this, and have the opportunity to spend a little time with old friends.

On the two Sundays I was there, Madeline and I went to mass, which was still said in Latin. When the offering plate was passed around, I was somewhat shocked when Madeline put a penny into it and promptly took out of the plate a halfpenny.

Hardly believing what I saw, I whispered to her, 'Madeline, that was terrible.'

To which she replied, 'Well, He's got more money than me!'

I couldn't argue the fact.

After saying goodbye to my friends, I was returned to St. Anne's by train and later placed in another domestic position at Kingswood in the County of Surrey, supposedly to look after two small children.

It was another disastrous situation, which I knew in my heart would not last long. Not only did I take care of the children but also every cleaning job in the house. In addition, the replacement cost of every item I nervously broke was deducted from my low wages, so some weeks I ended up with but a few pennies. It seemed I was forever to be reminded of the glass broken in the refectory years ago, the replacement cost of which, of course, I had never paid.

WAR WORK

In 1941, it became mandatory for all persons over the age of sixteen to register at the local Labour Exchange. Eager to get involved in whatever was necessary to help the war effort, and also seizing the opportunity to get out of another worthless domestic situation, I registered immediately at the Banstead Exchange in the County of Surrey. I was promptly told to report for work at Vickers-Armstrong, an aircraft factory in Weybridge, Surrey.

Arriving at the factory alongside a number of other young girls, I was given an application form to fill out, which I duly completed to the best of my ability. After a short interview, the Welfare Officer arrived and advised me that board and lodgings had been arranged for me within a short distance from the factory.

The basic wages were low, and the only means of earning extra money was by increasing one's daily production output, for which a weekly bonus was paid. Work entailed using an electric drill for making holes in four-foot-long strips of metal that were used on aircraft. I didn't like the drill; it was noisy and cumbersome to hold and I was forever dropping it. Having had no prior experience in this type of work, I soon found that the industrial gloves I wore had more holes drilled into them than the metal strips. My hands were always red and scratched and the torn skin took ages to heal, due to lack of hand cream, and the cold.

The shop foreman, Mr. Morrison, a short stocky man, normally so patient with his "new recruits", was much chagrined to be constantly replacing my holed gloves with new ones. He proceeded to show me how to get a better grip on the drill but, like a jellied eel, it continued to slither out of my hand, with the greatest of ease.

The location of my lodgings, arranged through the Welfare Officer at the factory, necessitated a short bus ride to work. My tiny bedroom, always so bitterly cold, was in a neat, small bungalow owned by an elderly couple. Food was scarce, and there was never enough to whet the appetite when served breakfast or evening meal. If meat was ever

The author, Carrie Marshall, at age 18, working in War Work.

available, it was so thinly sliced, a sneeze would have blown it off the plate! I could hardly make ends meet; my board absorbed most of my earnings. I was overwhelmed by this new experience of poverty; it was not what I had bargained for.

Lunchtime at the factory consisted of one slice of dry bread, and a beef cube dissolved in hot water. The water was heated in a tiny metal kettle on top of a small electric ring, borrowed from one of my co-workers who used it for making tea. Meals cooked in the Works' canteen I simply couldn't afford. Not surprisingly, and without doubt due to lack of sustenance, a co-worker one day found me slumped across the work bench, fortunately without the electric drill in my hand.

I was taken to the first-aid room where the Works' doctor advised a period of rest and a change of job. Returning to the factory a few weeks later, my duties became lighter and I was able to handle a sitting down job of hammering serial numbers onto aircraft components. Although the Welfare Officer managed to find me other accommodation, conditions of food or heat were no better there than the previous lodgings. Scarcity of food was even worse in this house, some days not even a slice of bread or a single potato could be found in the larder. We went to work hungry.

The girls from St. Anne's, when they reached sixteen years of age, were sent out "into the world" to work, usually in some domestic, menial labour role, as happened to me. Not surprisingly, most of the "employers" were convents, institutions and other enterprises owned and operated by the Catholic Church. The wages were so poor, and the conditions so bleak, that the young people became essentially cheap slave labour for the Church. Some of the girls became maids, living in parish priests' houses. The orphan boys were placed in labour positions – at miserably low wages – in farms run by the Christian Brothers. Yet there were too many children coming out of the institutions – far more than even the Church's commercial empire could absorb. The solution was to ship thousands of children overseas to work as farm help for Catholic families.

My brother William had been brought up at St. Mary's Convent, Gravesend in the County of Kent.

My older sister Margaret (who had been raised at St. Anne's as "Kathleen Brandon") worked in a convent in Worthing, Sussex. Elizabeth had been sent to Liphook, Hampshire, to look after small children. She would devote her life to caring for infants and the elderly, mostly in the London area. We kept in touch annually, meeting at the "Old Girls Reunion Day" held each summer at St. Anne's. One topic we always discussed was: "where was our brother?"

The answer appeared in 1943. William sought us out at a reunion day at St. Anne's. Like most of the boys leaving St. Mary's, he worked on a farm in Bletchingly, Sussex, run by the Christian Brothers. William, 17 years of age, left the farm and enlisted in the Royal Navy, preferring to risk his life fighting the Germans on the high seas over labouring on the farm, for poor wages.

Alas, William held no information about our parents – he knew less than we did, which was very, very little.

WEDDING BELLS

At nineteen years of age, I weighed a fraction over eighty pounds and was as "skinny as a beanpole". In 1944, a handsome blond, in his mid-twenties, came into my life. Clarence 'Larry' Whitehead was nearly six feet tall, and was born in Glamorganshire, South Wales. He was a mechanical engineer, exempt from the armed forces due to being employed in important War Work. We would be together for fifty-five years, until his death in 1999. We were introduced by a friend at Walton-on-Thames, Surrey, in the *'High-Spot'*, which was nicknamed the "half-a-crown-hop", as this is what it cost to gain admittance.

We started to court each other and, within six months, decided to get married. I had no idea that in order to undertake this ceremony, an obstacle would need to be overcome. To my consternation, I was told I would need the consent of the local magistrate as I was under the legal age and had no known parents from whom I could obtain permission to marry.

The dreaded day arrived for me to appear at Chertsey Assizes in Surrey. Feeling apprehensive, I stood before the magistrate hardly daring to breathe but, much to my surprise, the ordeal went smoother than I had anticipated. The magistrate simply wanted to know the "whys and wherefores" of who had brought me up and where I was currently living. He was kind with his questioning, and consent to marry was duly granted. Leaving the courtroom, feeling elated, I could hardly wait to give my fiancé the exciting news.

The wedding date was set for the afternoon of July 29. I was dressed in a long, white gown borrowed from a co-worker named Eileen, who was also one of my bridesmaids. The ceremony took place in the Catholic church at Walton-on-Thames. The service began at two o'clock and finished at exactly ten minutes past the hour. Lighted candles, mass or holy communion was forbidden due to the groom being non-Catholic.

Shortly after our wedding I suggested to my husband that perhaps he might like to visit the orphanage in Kent as he had never been there. Far too embarrassed and ashamed of the stigma attached to my childhood to discuss the full details with him during our courtship, I thought he would be interested in seeing the place in which I was raised.

It wasn't, of course, the first time I had been back to St. Anne's since being discharged in 1941. I tried returning, yearly, in order to meet up with some of the "old girls" on Reunion Day, normally held mid-summer. It also provided me with an opportunity of seeking out a staff member or nun in the hope of extracting the tiniest piece of information from them about my parents. Inevitably, though, their answers to any questions were always the same: 'You don't want to know, child – let sleeping dogs lie.' A pat on the head, that was all I got!

Inquiries to the Southwark Diocese in London had met with no better responses; in fact, their philosophy was much worse: 'Why do you want to know? We can't give you any details; we don't know.'

Doors closed! It appeared as though the attitude of that era was to blame the children for the actions of their parents. The authorities and nuns treated us with unjustified contempt and referred to us as "shameful hussies". I could almost hear them saying this as I left their offices at 59 Westminster Bridge Road, London.

The urge to know my parents, and the frustration in the not-knowing, was exasperating and distressed me to the point of paranoia. I was determined that regardless of anyone wanting to help or not, I would one day find out the truth about my parents and my own identity. I wasn't to realize then, the enormity of pain and anxiety I would suffer because of my determination to learn the truth.

At nineteen years of age, when I travelled into London, every journey I made left me groping helplessly down dark narrow streets that I found frightening. The pavements were dirty and slippery, due to continual rain, and to get from one street to the other was like going through endless tunnels. From the bombings of London mountains of rubble could be seen piled everywhere and if one did not tread carefully, there was every possibility of falling into a bomb crater.

It was a formidable task for even the healthiest of people to undertake, and I wondered many times if I had the strength to continue this relentless search for my family, which I found so mentally and physically debilitating. At each and every turn of events when visiting the East End of London, areas in which I was now becoming quite familiar, I began to have doubts whether my parents were still alive or if they had been evacuated to some other part of the country – particularly since a war was still raging and the bombings had destroyed many buildings in London, killing thousands of people.

My husband and I scheduled a Saturday for visiting St. Anne's and caught the early train from Walton-on-Thames in the County of Surrey, to London. As was usual on the Waterloo line, uniformed men were everywhere, packed tight into the compartments. No seats were available so we stood in the corridor the full length of the journey. When the train pulled into Waterloo we managed to disembark, unscathed, before the panic of "flying" rifles, kitbags and bodies in khaki broke loose.

Crossing over to the Charing Cross line, we boarded a train to Kent and got off at Orpington station. Walking hand-in-hand down Station Approach Road, we turned right at the bottom of it and went under a small railway bridge. A few yards along on the left side of the road was Orpington Hospital, and across on the right side was the tall, ugly-looking building of the orphanage. I wondered how the nuns would react to my bringing a strange man into their sanctuary.

Standing near the edge of the roadside, silently staring up at this formidable grey institution, my husband piped up, 'It looks just like a prison.'

I explained to him that the small, bare windows in the front of the building were the large dormitories, and that at the rear of the building the school-house, playground and the refectory could be found.

We walked up the long avenue to the entrance of the orphanage, over which stood a holy statue. I told him that the big, front oak door was strictly used for important visitors. Pausing at the entrance, we decided best to enter by the church side door, which led into a small passageway.

At the top of the passageway was another door that took us into the long, marble corridor. As we started walking along the corridor we noticed several nuns were coming out of the chapel area, so we stopped to speak to them. With a feeling of great pride, I introduced my husband to them.

Our visit was short – unfulfilled you might say. Homeward-bound to Surrey, my husband indicated he was not impressed.

Over the years, gradually gaining confidence in myself, I persisted in asking endless questions about my parents, many times going back to St. Anne's and the Southwark Diocese in London. My visits, painful and very tiring, proved negative regardless to whom I spoke, be it bishop, nuns or priest. I was forced to live with their on-going philosophy of "let sleeping dogs lie", which of course, was not the answer. The authorities, with lips sealed, kept the doors firmly closed for forty years.

Carrie, Margaret and Elizabeth
meet at Richmond Park, Surrey, in 1945.

EMIGRATE TO CANADA

As World War Two came to an end in 1945, I decided I would, of necessity, have to go for further education if I was to secure a better lifestyle. This I did by going to college and taking a secretarial course. After completing the course, I then applied for a secretarial position and found that the opportunities available to me were far greater than those forced upon me, as a domestic servant – that training being all the Catholic authorities were prepared to give to any girl when leaving the orphanage.

I carried on with my career as a secretary up to the time of my daughter's birth in 1955. A year later, due to my husband being made redundant at work, he decided we should emigrate to Canada!

After booking our passage we left Southampton on a rusty old Greek ship, the *SS Columbia*, an ex-troop ship from 1914, weighing seven thousand tons.

The voyage across to Canada was the most horrendous ten days of my life, and even after paying the full fare, the service we were given was shocking, to say the least! What alarmed most of the passengers more than anything was the state of the ship itself, for on going onto the boat deck and looking at the lifeboats we were appalled to find they were bolted down to the deck, so what chance of survival did we have if anything should happen to the ship? Nobody was more thankful than I to get off that floating wreck, as we docked in Wolfe's Cove, Quebec, on a bitterly cold day.

On arriving in Canada we journeyed to Toronto, and met up with some English friends whom we had known in the early 1950s. We

My husband, Clarence Whitehead, and I.

stayed in Ontario for two and a half years but, alas, found we couldn't adapt to the lifestyle of the big city, as we had always been used to the countryside and missed the quiet life. After much discussion my husband and I decided, reluctantly, to return to England; the main reason being the oppressive heat of the summer, and the bitterly cold winters, which we could not endure.

Returning home my husband was fortunate enough to be able to secure his previous job with his old company, who were in need of a representative in the Kent district. Ironically, we found ourselves purchasing a house in the Orpington area where I was brought up as a child at St. Anne's – the memory of which still haunted me.

After settling down I decided, once more, this was an opportunity for me to carry on with the search for my family. Being back in England enabled me to go to St. Catherine's House in London and thoroughly search the records. The births, marriages and deaths records had now been transferred from Somerset House to St. Catherine's.

However, again, I seemed to draw a blank, for after travelling back and forth from Kent to the record office in London on numerous occasions, it dawned on me that without the vital information I required concerning my parents' marriage, I would be unable to get any further ahead. Nevertheless, I was reluctant to give up my quest in the search for my family and felt compelled to explore every avenue that was open to me, on the chance that on one of my visits to the record office I would find some small item of information that would help me reach my goal.

As time passed and my regular visits to the record office became a routine and I still seemed to be getting nowhere, I was most surprised, one day, to receive a letter in 1960 from a Legal Aid Officer of the Royal Naval Barracks in Portsmouth, requesting my help in obtaining a birth certificate for my brother William, who was in the Navy. It appeared they wanted to draft him out to a naval station abroad and couldn't do so unless he had a passport, for which they needed his birth certificate. This was quite a shock to me, for on reflection I thought if the Navy was asking me for information concerning my brother's birth certificate, what chance would I have of getting the information I required about my family. Surely they were in a far better position to obtain information than I? Hoping it would assist my brother in getting his birth certificate, I forwarded a copy of mine to the Royal Navy.

After further correspondence from the Naval Legal Aid Officer, it transpired that the details required for my brother's birth certificate were mainly taken from my own, and my two sisters, so my hopes of gleaning any information from the Naval authorities were dashed once again.

Shortly after this episode, a further crisis occurred when the firm employing my husband was taken over by a larger company, with the result he was made redundant. Once again he decided to uproot the family and return to Canada, hoping for a better life.

RETURN TO CANADA

After living back in England for seven years, we were rather surprised to learn from the authorities at Canada House in London that in order for us to return to Canada, we would have to re-emigrate and repeat the immigration process all over again. At last, having followed all procedures, we arrived back in Canada in April of 1967 – Canada's Centennial Year.

Once settled again in Ontario, we were both amazed and pleased to discover that many improvements had happened since we left in 1959. Urban development was very much on the upward swing with new plazas and housing estates springing up everywhere. The economy was booming and jobs were easy to find. I determined that, once financially stable, come what may, I would return to England at least every other year to search for the information about my family that had eluded me so far. This I did faithfully.

It was on one of my visits to Britain – which had taken on the feeling of pilgrimages – that I decided to return yet again to the orphanage in Orpington. On this particular visit in 1974, I went to see May Lyle who used to be in charge of the workroom and, after sixty years of service, was now retired having reached a grand old age. She invited me into her tiny bedroom, situated on the lower floor in a small staff building close to the church, and sitting on her bed we began to chat about the "old days". Never without a sewing needle in her hand, she showed me some beautiful silk flowers she was working on, which were exquisite and colourful. Speaking in a soft voice, she told me she knew my mother and used to watch her from her workroom windows taking her three little girls, hand-in-hand down the long avenue away from the orphanage on her way back to London. She said my mother had been back and forth three times to the orphanage to take us home, and the third time the Catholic authorities called a halt and ruled: 'no more!'

'It was the last time she saw her children and it must have broken her poor heart to have to give you all up. She tried to keep you, she really did try,' May Lyle whispered.

Totally unprepared for this piece of news which had come from May Lyle quite spontaneously, I was not only saddened but also deeply shocked, because despite persistent questioning about my parents for many years everyone I approached at St. Anne's or the Catholic authorities in London remained as tight-lipped as ever. I felt like crying! How could they do this to me and deny me information about my parents? Over the years, at the orphanage, the nuns told me I was an orphan – a "nothing" when all the time they knew I had a mother who had visited me during my early years!

Recovering from the shock and sitting quietly for a minute or two, I then asked her if she remembered me sitting outside the workroom door listening to the music coming from her gramophone.

She replied, 'Yes, very well.'

Leading from the marble hall were long staircases going up to the dormitories. Another staircase led down to the workroom. May Lyle obviously enjoyed music, especially the classics, and often she would take out her gramophone and play records on it, or turn on her small radio and listen to the news.

Besotted with music at an early age, I would make my way downstairs and sit as close as I could to the workroom door. My arms folded across my knees, and my head in my lap, there I would listen to the sounds coming from behind the closed door. One day, so engulfed was I listening to the music, I didn't hear the door open. May Lyle came out of the workroom and caught me sitting on the stairs.

I looked up at her and shyly said, 'I like the music, Miss.'

She smiled, understandingly, I thought, and went back inside the workroom, closing the door gently behind her. I'm sure she knew I often sat on the stairs many times spellbound by the music, but she never spoke one word to me; it appeared a secret bond had developed between us.

This was the last time I saw May Lyle, for whom I always held a certain affection. Of all the staff she was the only one I could remember who often smiled. She retired in 1955 after sixty years service at St. Anne's. She passed away when she was well into her eighties and was buried in a small cemetery near the playing fields. Her kindness to me has never been forgotten. A great amateur photographer she took many snaps of the children as they were growing up and, but for her interest in photography, I would not be in possession of a photograph of my sisters and me, when we were young.

Life in Canada carried on as usual, and despite my on-going visits to England in the desperate search for information regarding my parents, the doors were still firmly closed. If my parents were still alive, they would be getting very old. Time was running out.

On a visit to St. Catherine's House in 1983, I met a man named Mr. Wakelin, a librarian from Hampshire, and during a discussion with him I explained the difficulties I was experiencing in tracing family records. He suggested that I write to a Lord Teviot at the House of Lords in London, as he was known to be interested in genealogy and he might be helpful to me in my search for family. This I did, without delay, and although I sent Lord Teviot various pieces of information, together with a reply addressed envelope and a photograph of myself, he did not respond to my letter. So once more I was disillusioned but was still determined to carry on, come what may. To give up now when I had come this far, was unquestionable.

Due to my husband's poor health in 1987, he was advised by his doctor to retire from work, so we decided to move from Ontario to British Columbia, where the climate was more temperate.

When we had settled down into our new home, I was eager to search the whereabouts of the local library and found it was within close proximity of where we now lived. One day, while browsing through the books on one of the shelves in the library I came across a book entitled

'In Search of your British and Irish Roots' written by Angus Baxter, an English Genealogist living at Lakefield, Ontario.

I took the book home with me and was so interested with the genealogy information contained therein, that I scrutinized every detail from cover to cover not once, but twice, determined not to overlook any knowledge that would put me on the right trail and, perhaps, open the doors which had forever been locked against me.

I resolved there and then to write to the author of the book and explain briefly how I had been searching for my parents for the past forty years, to no avail. I described how I had travelled from my home in Surrey up to worn-torn London, looking for any help I could get from the Catholic authorities, which was of little or no consequence. The perilous journeys I undertook travelling across London to the various record offices, having at times to make a dash for the nearest air raid shelter as the warning sounded in order to get to safety as the German bombers came droning over the capital, to drop their loads of death and destruction. All of this I was prepared to endure in my desperate quest to find my parents. Each time I approached the Catholic authorities they would come out with the same old time-worn phrase, "let sleeping dogs lie". I felt as though I was banging my head against a brick wall, as deep down, I had the impression that the knowledge I required was known to them but for some obscure reason they were not willing to divulge it to me. Could it be there were answers that would rebound on them, so they were afraid to expose the truth?

I pointed out in my letter to Mr. Baxter that my search over such a lengthy period of time had been fruitless, and no doubt the trail was now long cold. All I could offer him by way of documentation was a baptismal certificate which I obtained from the parish priest in Walworth, London, at the Church of the English Martyrs, where I was baptized.

After posting my letter off to him I waited in anticipation, hoping against hope I would receive a reply. As the days passed I began to get anxious, wondering whether my letter to him appealing for his help had fallen on deaf ears when, out of the blue, a couple of weeks later, the long-awaited letter arrived.

Tearing open the envelope with nervous fingers, I stared at the letter dated April 12, 1988, and couldn't believe my good fortune when he stated: 'Normally – as you may imagine – I just do not have the time to do anything about personal problems such as yours – I lecture a great deal and am also in the midst of writing another book and six articles a year for *'Heritage Quest'*. However, every now and then someone gives me a problem which touches my hard heart and yours is such a one. I will do all I can to help you.'

He then went on to listing various questions about my parents, my history before I was nineteen, and 'to sit down, rack your brains, give me the answers to my questions, send me a copy of your birth certificate if you have one. Tell me the exact date in 1925 when you were born and tell me how you know this.'

He added, 'I can understand your frustration and will do all I can to help – but I have no magic touch and may not discover any more than you.'

In response to Mr. Baxter's letter I endeavoured to answer his questions as best as possible, and enclosed copies of my brother and sisters' birth certificates, along with my own, hoping they would be of some help to him. It was impossible for me to give him any firm details of my parents' background, as I simply had no knowledge of them whatsoever.

In Mr. Baxter's following letter dated June 6, 1988 his opening remarks were that he had nothing positive to report. He had visited England in May 1988, for four weeks, and had spent hours at the headquarters of The Society of Genealogists in London checking through directories for the whole of London for the period of 1918–1930 for any record of my parents as either owners or tenants of a house or apartment. There were none.

Mr. Baxter's next visit was to The Public Record Office at Kew in the County of Surrey, where he spent the day searching through Naval records of my father, but found nothing positive. He then decided to put certain enquiries in motion: a search of London's Poor Law records for the Walworth area; a record of Naval enlistment of my father since 1891, whether he was a regular sailor, or whether he was a stoker during the 1914-1918 war; a check by a contact of his at St. Catherine's House on the birth of either of my parents in the period 1880–1890. In fairness, he could not ask for a longer search at this stage.

'We will see what comes out of these enquiries,' he wrote.

After further correspondence with Mr. Baxter, who had been so generous in giving freely his invaluable time on my behalf, the floodgates finally opened, and through his contacts in England I received information about my father who had served as a Chief Petty Officer in the Royal Navy, along with his service record dating back to 1902, from the Ministry of Defence at Hayes in the County of Middlesex.

As the New Year of 1989 approached I felt something positive would be happening and, in due course, on January 24 I received news from Mr. Rudall (Mr. Baxter's contact in London) that he was sending my parents' birth and marriage certificates to me! Overcome with emotion, I knew at long last all the perseverance, which caused me great anxiety, had been worthwhile.

Elated at my good fortune in receiving this news of my parents, I decided to make another journey from British Columbia to England as I was more eager than ever to see the tiny village of Lydd in the County of Kent, the birthplace of my father. I didn't realize at the time that this undertaking would, at some later date, bring the most astounding news, along with the biggest surprise of my life.

Flying back to the UK, I landed at Gatewick Airport, to be met there by my brother William, whereupon we took a taxi to his home in Hampshire, travelling through some of the most beautiful countryside of southern England. After settling down at my brother's house, we discussed our plans to visit various places of interest to us, in particular Father's birthplace at Lydd in the County of Kent.

Angus Baxter wrote to the *Chatham, Rochester and Gillingham News*, the *Kent Evening Post*, and the local newspaper in Lydd, making a general enquiry on the subject of ancestor hunting, mentioning only my father's name, place of origin and Naval service. In response, we were put in touch with a cousin who had apparently, as a child, while her father was serving in the Army during the Second World War, lived with my grandfather Edward Rutley Marshall in Lydd, Kent, with her mother, brother and sister. This family was totally unaware of my existence.

My cousin, whose name is Wendy and lives at Bexhill in the County of Sussex, kindly offered to show my brother and me around the village of

Lydd as she knew the area well from living with Grandfather. Meeting up with her the following day, we were taken to this delightful little village and through the lovely old Saxon church, parts of which date back to 1557. It was here that we were shown the graves of some of our ancestors, one of whom was a Lieutenant J.D. Godfrey, R.N., D.S.O., of the *HMS Arethusa*. During the Battle of Helegolan Bight in World War One, Godfrey was credited with firing the torpedo that sank the German battleship *Blucher*. For this, he was awarded the Distinguished Service Order.

While travelling around Lydd with my cousin and brother we were introduced to the Parochial Secretary of the Church, a lady by the name of Dorothy Beck, who at that time was in the process of working on the Marshall family tree. This timely event came about because her husband's friend was related to the Marshalls of Lydd and requested this favour from her.

After a lengthy discussion on the family's history it was apparent, to both parties, that the information we had exchanged was startling, to say the least! According to Dorothy Beck's records of the Marshall tree, there was no indication that my father had any children at all, which left us thoroughly puzzled.

Before taking our leave, Mrs. Beck put me in touch with David Wright, a researcher in family history, living at Whitstable in the County of Kent, saying, 'I'm sure he will help you.'

Although I was anxious for more details, I could not help but harboured some nagging feelings of sadness and shame about why my mother allowed my sisters, brother and I to be put into an orphanage without seemingly any thought for us. Learning more might not lessen my grief as to the underlying reasons for this sad episode in my life.

The time passed all too quickly for me as my holiday in England ended, and so in March 1989 I returned to my home in Canada satisfied with what I had accomplished.

While unpacking my luggage the following day, I came across the envelope that Dorothy Beck had given me, with the address of David

Wright, and thought it would be an opportune time to write to him to see if he could unravel any of the mystery that surrounded my family.

Seizing this opportunity, I wrote to David Wright asking if he could possibly obtain my mother's death certificate for me, which was a problem due to the fact that I could not provide St. Catherine's House in London with the date or year in which she died. When requesting this piece of information from David Wright I had no idea of the repercussions that were to follow, leading me to the one person who was to give me all the news I wanted to hear concerning my mother.

Up to this time, in spite of searching for over forty years, all I had managed to obtain thus far was my parents' birth and marriage documents, so I requested him to search the records to find *any* personal information he could on my mother. In particular I was desperate to secure her death certificate. This, I knew, would enable me to see in which part of England she lived at the time of her death, and where she was buried.

As the days lengthened into weeks and there was no correspondence from Mr. Wright, I began to get extremely anxious and the thought struck me that, being so many thousands of miles away, literally across the other side of the world, it was a case of "out of sight, out of mind". Feeling rather despondent, I toyed with the idea of telephoning my brother in Hampshire to see if he could help by visiting Mr. Wright in person but, on second thought, discretion being the better part of valour, I decided against this move. However desperate I was to press on ahead with my search, I resolved to wait and see.

A month later, patience it seems paid off for me, as when taking the mail from the box there to my relief and joy was the letter I had long awaited from David Wright. Thanking me for my letter, he apologized for being so long in replying, due to pressure of work. Then without further ado, he got right down to business by requesting a fee of one hundred and twenty-five pounds sterling, for a two-day search for my mother's death certificate, providing I forward him her birth and marriage documents, which I had successfully obtained through Mr. Rudall in London.

My father's death certificate was made possible through the kindness of the late Angus Baxter, when he had advertised in the *Chatham,*

Rochester and Gillingham News, which was responded to by a Mr. Cyril Scott who lived at Strood, Rochester, Kent.

In Mr. Scott's letter to Angus Baxter, he stated he knew my father, since a boy of eleven, as Ted Marshall and that Mr. Marshall had worked at the Royal Naval Barracks, Chatham, since leaving the service. He went on to say that my father had been dead for many years and his wife Sarah returned to live in Devonport, Plymouth, to join the rest of her family.

Mr. Scott's closing comments were, 'As far as I am aware, Ted Marshall had no children.'

In thanking Mr. Scott for providing me with this valuable information, I let the matter rest there. However, a week or two later I was dumbfounded to receive another letter from him, enclosing a certified copy of my father's death certificate, which I had not requested of him. He must have sensed the urgency in my previous letter for information of my father, as he took it upon himself to write to the Register of Births, Deaths and Marriages, Chatham, Kent, for this document, enclosing the required fee of five pounds sterling.

It is not necessary for me to relate what it meant to me in receiving this certificate, which a complete stranger had taken it in his heart to achieve on my behalf, but if I had only met someone like Cyril Scott years ago when searching for my parents, my ordeals would surely have been minimized.

Sadly, when visiting England in 1989, I made a special journey to see Cyril Scott at Strood, Rochester, as I personally wanted to shake his hand and thank him for going to the trouble of getting my father's death certificate. However, upon calling at his house, I was informed by his wife, May, that he had passed away a few weeks earlier.

In June 1989, at last, the news I had waited for arrived with the next letter from David Wright. He enclosed my mother's death certificate along with a copy of my father's Will, which I had not thought to ask for. Together with these documents I was surprised to see another death certificate for my mother's fourth husband, a Thomas Martin, whose marriage to my mother in 1928 had been confirmed earlier by Mr. Rudall. There was a further request by Mr. Wright, for an additional seventy-five pounds sterling, to cover extended labour hours. In reply to Mr. Wright, I thanked him for his excellent work in furnishing me with all these documents.

Having now secured details of my father's Naval records from the Ministry of Defence, Hayes, Middlesex, and family history of the Marshalls from Dorothy Beck, the Parochial Secretary of All Saints Church, Lydd, Kent, I resolved to pursue mother's side of the family hoping this would satisfy the anguish, heartache and pain that lay within me for the past forty-odd years. Perhaps it would finally give me peace of mind in the knowledge I had family – and that I really was someone and not just a piece of flotsam as the Catholic authorities would have me, drifting along on the ocean of life.

In my letter to Mr. Wright, I asked him to search the Ashby side of my family; this being the maiden name of my mother. Having mailed this off to him, I sat back quite pleased with myself, thinking it might eventually clear my last obstacle and that I was heading for the final chapter in my desperate quest for family history.

However, in a further letter from Mr. Wright dated July 2,1990 he stated, 'the details about your parents and brother and sisters, according to the photocopies, are indeed complex and mystifying at this stage. To start investigations would require three or four days work; the initial fee to cover these costs would be two hundred pounds sterling.'

My reply to Mr. Wright was to request that he go ahead with the search, realizing what a formidable task I had placed before him.

It would be September 10, 1990 before I received additional news from Mr. Wright and to be quite frank I didn't expect to hear too much from him concerning the Ashby family, as they seemed to have disappeared. Hastily opening the envelope, I withdrew from it four sheets of correspondence and in so doing, a folded document dropped out. Thinking this may relate to mother's family, I ignored it for the moment and continued to read the enclosed letter.

Suddenly, I stood transfixed and rooted to the spot. I couldn't believe what I had just read – it seemed preposterous. In his letter David Wright stated that, when checking for the Ashby family, he drew a blank so decided to try another avenue of search on the Marshall file, Mother's married name. After a final and colossal search he came up with the following birth index for a Rowland Charles Marshall born in London, January, 1919.

'This person appears to be a full and legitimate brother to yourself. Prolonged investigation may reveal his present whereabouts and that, I am sure, will lead to verbal proof of the background of your childhood. I imagine that if Rowland Charles Marshall is still alive, and can be traced, he may be able to say much more than we are able to surmise from documentary records, such as his birth certificate that I have forwarded to you.'

Regaining my composure after reading such astounding news, I hurriedly put on my coat, got into my car and drove over to my daughter's house which was a short distance away, to show her the letter.

Upon arrival, she took one look at me and said: 'Mother, what's up?'

I could hardly contain myself, as I handed the letter to her, saying, 'You won't believe it.'

Sitting myself down, I watched the expression on her face as her eyes moved from side to side while she read each line carefully.

Then, with a look of utter amazement spread over her face, she gasped: 'It's not possible, it's so unreal. Do you think someone is playing a joke on you, knowing you are constantly in search for family?'

In response to her question, I withdrew my brother's birth certificate from the envelope, saying, 'I don't think anyone would go to the trouble of forging an official document for a joke, do you?'

To say we were ecstatic, is to say the least! My excitement knew no bounds in the news that I had found a brother whose existence was totally unbeknown to me. I wondered, could he be alive, or am I too late because of his age? He could be long dead, or maybe killed during the last war.

All these possibilities were uppermost in my thoughts. Nevertheless, I decided to press on; the road had been too hard and long for me to stop now.

Without further delay I wrote to Joan Savage, a friend who lives at

Lydd, telling her the wonderful news I had received from David Wright: he had found a brother by sheer luck when checking the Marshall birth indexes at St. Catherine's House in London. I mentioned in my letter to Joan that a further fee of two hundred and fifty pounds sterling would be required if I wanted Rowland's whereabouts tracked down.

I asked for Joan's advice. In the light of this expense and the fact he would be seventy-two years of age at the time of writing, he could be long gone. Did she think it worthwhile pursuing this course of action or could she advise me on the best way to go about obtaining this information? Because Joan herself was extremely involved and interested in genealogy and had many successes over the years in tracing her own ancestors as well as those of her friends and other people who wrote to her for help, I was sure her advice on my efforts to find Rowland would be sound and prove positive.

I didn't have to wait long for Joan's reply. She suggested the best way to handle this, without too much expense involved, would be to write directly to the Salvation Army Headquarters in London. Their successful work in tracing missing relatives was known throughout the world. Joan went on to recommend I forward to them whatever particulars I had on my brother, plus a copy of his birth certificate.

By the way, she added, 'Don't forget to send them a donation as the work they undertake is for a worthy cause.'

Taking my friend's advice, I wasted no time in posting a letter off to the Salvation Army, pleading for their help. This, I hoped, would at least give me the vital news I so badly wanted, informing me of the whereabouts of a brother I had never known.

As the days passed into weeks and lengthened into months, and time slowly dragged on, I began to wonder if I would ever get any response to my plea for help from the Salvation Army. After almost three months had gone by and Christmas was drawing ever nearer, I busied myself sending off greeting cards to my friends and relations overseas.

One day, on picking up my letters from the mail box, I was surprised to find a letter addressed to me with a Liverpool postmark on the envelope.

Rather puzzled, I thought to myself, 'Who do I know from that part of England? The only time I saw Liverpool was when I joined a ship there, to re-emigrate to Canada in 1967, aboard the *Empress of Canada*.'

Opening up the envelope I withdrew a Christmas card from inside and stared at the message on the front of it which said, *'To a Wonderful Sister'*.

I had already received a card from my brother William in Hampshire and, rather puzzled, I thought I had someone else's mail. But on opening out the card I read, *'From your loving brother, Rowland.'*

Trembling with excitement, I stared at the card in my hand and knew, without doubt, it was positive proof that he was alive. Although the hand-writing was nervously scrawled, I could detect from it strokes of characteristic lines similar to those of my own. Turning to the enclosed letter I slowly read the address, hoping there would be a telephone number to enable me to make immediate contact with him; alas, there was none.

Picking up my telephone directory I called the overseas operator in England to see if Rowland was listed in the Merseyside 'phone book, but the operator informed me there was no such listing for a Rowland Charles Marshall. However, he added, 'His number could be ex-directory.'

Determined not to waste any precious time, overjoyed as I was at receiving a beautiful Christmas card from Rowland, I 'phoned William in Hampshire to tell him I had heard from Rowland. William asked if I would let him have Rowland's address so he could write to him immediately.

Christmas was but a couple of days away and, as was usual, my sisters Elizabeth (now living in Victoria) and Margaret (living in the State of Washington) came to spend the holiday with me. It was always a great time for us to spend Christmas and New Year together, along with my husband, daughter and her family, and enjoy the festive season with lots of lovely gifts, the trimmings off a fat turkey and homemade Christmas puddings. This was the one meal of the year we savoured and laboured over for hours between the chatting and laughter. These Christmas get-togethers were a joy to us all – we were family and that's all that mattered!

As the New Day of 1991 dawned I awoke to find we had all slept rather late into the morning, no doubt due to celebrating the festive season. The breakfast hour had long passed so I prepared a light lunch, hoping everyone would be fit enough to partake in the meal. We all went into the dining-room and as we sat dining the noise of the telephone ringing cut short our chatter.

Rising from my chair at the table, I glanced at the clock on the wall, which indicated one o'clock. I wondered who on earth this could be as we had already spoken to our many friends previously.

Picking up the receiver I said, 'Hello.'

The reply I heard all but threw me off balance, as a voice answered, 'Hello, Caroline, this is your brother Rowland.'

I couldn't believe my ears, I was so overwhelmed on hearing his voice for the first time that when I tried to speak the words just stuck in my throat. I called out to my sisters in the dining-room that Rowland was on the 'phone. As their heads turned towards me the look of utter amazement on both faces made me want to burst out laughing; their eyes popped out like organ stops, they were that surprised!

We chatted, excitedly, for a good half hour, trying to cram in the questions of a lifetime. I then handed the 'phone over to my sisters, so they could chat with him.

Finally, after promising he would call again soon, we all wished him a Happy New Year. He returned the compliment, and reluctantly rang off. Not wishing to replace the receiver, I held on until I heard a faint click of the line being switched off by the operator, and a wave of deep emotion welled up within, bringing forth a flood of tears.

On turning to face my sisters I found that they also had been overcome by the surprise telephone call from Rowland. While chatting together, we wondered how our newly-found brother had fared throughout his life. He had already told me, briefly, in our telephone conversation that he had lived with our mother from the age of thirteen until joining the Merchant Service and embarking on a sea career at the age of seventeen. To hear that he had actually lived with Mother for that period of his life, while the rest of us were pushed to one side, brought a feeling of great sadness to us all.

I asked myself, 'Why did Rowland go home, and not us?'

This question continued to haunt me, and as the months dragged by

My brother Rowland in his Merchant Marine dress uniform
and his bride Gladys at their wedding.

and our correspondence to each other became like a flood tide, I would try and glean as much information as possible from Rowland regarding our mother.

At this stage, however, he was trying to cope over the loss of his wife to whom he had been married for forty-six happy years. Gladys had passed away the previous August, after suffering from cancer. Although finding his sisters was a miracle which he never expected would happen to him in his lifetime, it was difficult for him to come to terms with his tragic loss. He was also preoccupied with the sale of his house, a most unpleasant task for him to undertake. Taking all these facts into consideration I felt it would be kinder if I didn't push too hard for the vital information I needed, and allow him to relate his story to me in his own good time. We had already made plans for him to come and stay with me in Canada for three months, when the time suited him, but nevertheless I felt an urge driving me on, to lift the veil of secrecy that still hung like a huge dark cloud over my life.

Eager for any tiny morsel of news about Mother, in further correspondence between us, I couldn't resist mentioning that she had remarried and, to all intents and purpose, abandoned us.

In his letter, replying to my questions, Rowland said he too failed to understand Mother's lack of parental care for her children but, then, we should not judge her too harshly as times were very hard for young women in the 1920s and her circumstances are unknown to us. So who are we to stand in judgement of her? Scant as the facts are concerning Mother, it must have been painful for him to relive the past.

'In conveying my thoughts,' he wrote, 'it might be better if I put the words into verse.'

Stemming the tears that threatened to cascade all over the paper, I slowly read the poem Rowland had sent me, and marvelled at the explicit way in which he wrote each verse trying in the kindest possible way, to see Mother's plight.

TANGLED WEB

O'er many years, it crossed my mind
Should I one day, my family find,
Dear Grandma told me, long ago
I've a secret, I'd like you to know,
You have a sister, my dear boy
Some day I know, she'll bring you joy.

Researchers, much to her delight
With information, brought to light,
A brother, she had never known
Who'd had to face the world alone,
Oh! what on earth had Mother done?
That she should hide, her first born son.

Or were to her, the fate's unkind
Suggesting, someone else she find,

In place of one that she now feared
So long ago, had disappeared,
So, my dear sister, feel no shame
Should Mother, really be to blame?

To know you fills my heart with joy
I heard your name when just a boy
A lifetime's pleasure, I have missed
Although to you, I did not exist
Maybe for Mother's peace of mind
Your brother was so hard to find

Today, my dear, I write to you
And really can't believe it's true,
A miracle, it must surely be
That you, by chance, discovered me,
We were so close, some years before
The day you left old England's shore.

Our search for roots has just begun
'Neath tangled webs that Mother spun,
She was so anxious from the start
That you and I, remain apart,
Her tracks she covered, oh so neat
In hoping we would never meet.

Throughout the war I fought at sea
While the Lord above watched over me,
To keep me safe out of harm's way
That we perhaps, should meet one day,
Great joy will fill this heart of mine
The day I meet you, Caroline.

This final verse, yes, just one more
Is somewhat longer than before,

We all have suffered I'm afraid
Because of tricks that Mother played
Some answers we may never find
Our mother left no clues behind
To questions, she no answers gave
Just took her secrets to the grave,
For her at least the troubles cease
Goodbye, dear Mother, rest in peace.

Time moved slowly forward, as I counted each day anxiously waiting to meet my older brother for the first time. In the meantime the correspondence and telephone calls continued at a startling speed; each time I was praying for more news of Rowland's past life. All he would say was he had a reasonable childhood, only to face a rather tough period surviving World War Two.

Eventually, the call I longed for came in late July 1991.

His message was short and to the point, as he told me in a voice filled with excitement, 'Caroline, I have sold my house, and have booked a flight, arriving Victoria airport at 3 p.m. on July 31. See you soon.'

I glanced at the calendar hanging in the kitchen. It was the 28th. My head began to spin, I felt so happy. Three days, I said to myself over and over again – it was so hard to believe, at long last, after all the years of frustration, and lies from the authorities, I would come face to face with a brother whose existence was unknown to me, and was the one person in the world who could provide me with reliable news of my mother.

The longest three days of my life were about to end, as I made preparations for Rowland's arrival. How I managed to get through lunch that day, I'll never know. Needless to say, I arrived at Victoria airport long before the plane was due, and proceeded to walk up and down impatiently, watching the hands of the clock, as they slowly moved to 3 p.m. Looking at the arrival screen and noting the plane from Vancouver

*July 31, 1991, after sixty-five years apart, Caroline
meets her long-lost brother Rowland for the first time,
in Victoria, BC, Canada.*

was due, I made a beeline for the window just in time to watch the tiny
island plane with its precious cargo touch down on the tarmac.

Waiting for the arrival doors to slide apart, I eagerly scanned all the
faces of people coming out. Suddenly, there he appeared, my newly-

found brother. Leaving his luggage, he rushed over to me with arms outstretched.

As we hugged each other, he whispered, 'This is the moment I have longed for all my life. I've been searching for you since I was a child.'

In a voice choked with emotion, and holding back the tears, I said, 'Miracles do happen.'

The three months Rowland and I spent together will be memories treasured forever. On most days we visited the numerous beautiful coves and beaches in and around Victoria, as well as other places of interest. In the light of the warm summer evening we would go for long walks on the beach, resting a while on a log facing out to sea, and chat about our family, in particular Mother. I couldn't fill my insatiable appetite for every scrap of news Rowland had of her; I wanted to hear the details now, rather than at some later date, knowing at this stage of my life, time was of the essence.

I told him of the hardships I had gone through in my younger days, my early marriage, finally emigrating to Canada, seeking for a better life.

Listening quietly to me, then speaking in a soft voice, he said, 'It's so sad that we didn't find each other years ago, as I could have made your life so much easier.'

Before returning home to England, Rowland and I agreed we would each write our own story, initially, I suppose, and for want of a better phrase – to "expose our souls". So much, in the past, has for one reason or the other, had to be concealed. My one fear, when going "out into the world", as the nuns so aptly put it, was the dread of some inquisitive mind finding out the stigma attached to my childhood background. It was a fear so deeply rooted it wasn't until the year 1990 – when news came about Rowland being alive – that I could bring myself to utter one word of my background to the person most dear to me, my daughter. It took all my courage to give her the details of my life, from the beginning. When I had finished, it was as though that solid block of concrete I stared down on in the bombed-out areas of the East End of London in 1944 had been lifted off me. Getting it out of my system left me exhausted.

My daughter told me she always felt there was a certain mystery surrounding me, as I never spoke of my family. However what she had just heard, neither surprised or shocked her. Some of the people were born a full century before, and the stories were lived in a very different era and a far-away land. I resolved to write down, for her, her children and grandchildren, all I'd discovered about our ancestors and the society in which they lived.

FAMILY CONNECTIONS

The scant information I have of John Coughtry Turner, my great-grandfather on my mother's side, indicates he was born 1820 in Chesham – a small town in the heart of the Chilterns. Chesham sits in the Chess Valley, with a population now of just over 20,000 souls.

Located in the County of Buckinghamshire, it is 28 miles north-west of London at the end of the Metropolitan line, and now forms part of Metroland. There have been settlers in Chesham from the Stone Age. In Roman Britain there were settlers here from 55 BC. A major villa at Latimer with a courtyard of over 30,000 square feet was built in the Chess Valley – on a major route to St. Albans, Hertfordshire.

In 1506, Thomas Harding became a martyr to his religion on White Hill. Chesham's most famous son owes his fame to Lewis Carroll whose character the Mad Hatter in *'Alice in Wonderland'* was based on Roger Crab, a hatter in Chesham in the seventeen century.

My great-grandfather, John Coughtry Turner, married a spinster named Mary Jane Bullen. They had three children. William was the eldest, Charlotte the second child, and the third was my grandmother, Elizabeth, born February 1869, at 6 York Street, Southwark, London. At the time of her birth, her father's occupation was given as Tanner Journeyman.

Elizabeth, the youngest child, lived with her parents who had then moved to 41 Swan Place, London, until she reached the age of sixteen. Her father, now an established Leather Dresser, carried on in the tannery business in London, and from his income afforded the family a comfortable lifestyle.

The few details I was able to extract from a first cousin about my great-grandfather indicated he was a hard-working man with high moral principles, which he impressed on each of his children. William went on to a position of Head Master in the rural area of Morden in the County of Surrey. Charlotte became a nurse.

Against the wishes of her parents, on reaching sixteen years of age, Elizabeth insisted on marrying her boyfriend whom she had known for only a short period of time. Her parents were of the opinion that he would not be a suitable husband for their daughter. Faced with this objection, Elizabeth threatened to elope with the boyfriend and take her chances head-on, without her parents' blessing – such was her determination to go ahead with her plans to marry. Her parents, who were devout Christians, were shocked by this turn of events in their daughter's life and were at a loss to understand where they may have gone wrong in her upbringing, for her to behave so rebelliously toward them. Sadly, a rift developed between them, and many years were to pass before Elizabeth would be welcomed back into the family fold.

The man who caused all this furore was named Frederick Proudfoot Ashby, a good-looking young man who joined the Royal Navy as a cabin boy at the age of seventeen, but did not rise to any responsible position by completion of service. He was twenty-one years of age when he married young Elizabeth in January 1885, at St. Peter's Church, Newington, London.

With good reason, Elizabeth's parents strongly disapproved of the marriage. Ashby had little background nor sufficient substance with which to earn a decent living to support a family. He was without academic or trade skills and appeared unable to hold a job for any length of time. Elizabeth's father could see the writing on the wall, and visions of hardships ahead. His predictions of poor prospects for his daughter were to come true. The old adage: 'you've made your bed, now lie on it,' must have been a hard lesson to swallow for Elizabeth – who had enjoyed every home comfort as a child. Yet, the deed was done, there was no turning back.

During the early years of their marriage she gave birth in succession to ten children – six daughters and four boys, two of whom died young within a period of two years of each other.

In the Victorian era, antibiotics and other medicines were unavailable to children suffering from smallpox, diphtheria and other known yet untreatable illnesses. The result was that many infants died at an early age, causing untold misery, anxiety and heartbreak to many poor families. Bad sanitation, said to be the main cause for many of the diseases, was prevalent during this period. The common people's logic of 'one mouth less to feed' sounds callous to us, but did not to them. The question uppermost in the minds of those people who lived in abject poverty, was a need to exist, by fair means or foul. The amount of food available to a family was governed by the husband's earnings, which determined if they could make ends meet.

In the early nineteenth century, only Dickens himself could adequately describe the appalling housing conditions in which working class families lived. The biggest fear of poverty was the lack of money with which to pay the rent. Failure to pay the landlord meant they would surely end up in the workhouse. Such was the predicament of these unfortunate people, facing their never-ending struggle to survive.

Life was far from easy for my grandmother, who faced a daunting task of rearing eight children, while trying to make ends meet. The meagre wage Grandfather brought home from work, where he was employed as a Wireworker, was hardly sufficient to feed a large family. Few, if any, pennies were left in the "kitty", and the thought of luxury however slight, never entered her head.

Much to Grandmother's credit, unlike millions of other mothers or parents who allowed their children to be taken away for reasons of poverty or because they were unable to cope with the strain of child-rearing, she kept all of her eight children at home and brought them up to be God-fearing Christians. Fully aware that the rift between herself and her family would take years to heal, any thought of asking her parents for guidance or help of any kind, was out of the question. They simply and stubbornly would not accept Frederick Proudfoot Ashby into the family. Nor any of his children. And that was that!

UNCLES AND AUNTS –
GROWING UP IN A WORLD OF HATS

Of Grandmother's six daughters, Ada Florence was her first child, born in 1886, when Grandmother was only 17. The second, Caroline, came into this world in 1888. Her third child, Lilian Mary, 1891. Then Rose Eveline, 1896. Another child, Nellie, born 1898, and Marie, in 1899.

Of her four sons, Frederick was born in 1901, William John, 1903, Robert Edward, 1905 and Ernest Victor, 1907. Frederick and William John passed away when infants.

These were all my aunts and uncles, with the exception of Grandmother's second daughter, my mother Caroline, born in 1888. Their children were my first cousins. Sadly, I knew nothing of these relatives until 1994. A childhood potentially rich in family relationships had been denied me – and rudely replaced by the cold, often-cruel life in an orphanage.

From conversations with cousins in the past decade, I learned that Grandmother encouraged her children to be self-reliant and taught her daughters the art of using a sewing needle from an early age. The children spent their childhood growing up in the Bermondsey area, in the East End of London. The house in which they lived, though small, was always kept spotlessly clean. Each child quickly learned, 'there is a place for everything.' Tidiness was part of their everyday routine, strictly adhered to, at all times.

When daily schoolwork was done and their household duties completed, the girls would sit in the tiny, neatly-kept front room parlour, otherwise reserved for visitors. There they would sew many large hats with colourful dried flowers and Victorian lace used to decorate the crown and brim. While sewing under Grandmother's ever-watchful eye, they would sing or chat happily with one another. Looking back over the years these were their happy childhood memories, giving them a feeling of family togetherness and a sense of belonging they would long remember.

After putting the finishing touch to a hat, each daughter would hand it to Grandmother who would examine it carefully, looking for any fault. Satisfied with the result of this creation of beauty, a broad smile would spread across her face and, in turn, she would nod her approval and praise each of her girls for work well done. It wasn't often the hats were returned for alteration – such was Grandmother's skill with the sewing needle and the art of teaching it.

To Grandmother, activities that wasted time were never allowed to develop in her smoothly-run household. Every minute counted. Also important to her was the thrifty use of materials. Whenever pieces of fabric or lace were left over from the finished hats, these treasured items were stored in a box in the kitchen cupboard, in readiness for use on the next new set of hats. It was unthinkable to throw anything out that could be of the slightest value. Her girls now expertly trained, Grandmother, with a feeling of anticipation and an urge to surge ahead, set about making plans for her next endeavour.

With the matter of survival forever strong in her mind, an idea developed that if there was any way in which she could sell the hats, extra money would help in satisfying her growing family's appetites. It would also supplement her husband's small wage, on which she struggled to make ends meet. The thought of bringing in extra pennies and sixpences was tantalizing to the point of allowing her senses to run wild, with thoughts of instant wealth. She toyed with the idea for days about how to go about making this first important step. Finally, as though directed by some being from above urging her on, she decided the time had come to show off and market her beautiful Victorian hats.

Knowing her neighbours and having made many friends over the years, she asked two of the ladies living close by to give her an honest opinion about the hats, and if they would be interested in buying one. While the hats were being examined from crown to brim, Grandmother's thoughts were traversing at an alarming speed through her head.

'I'm not giving them away,' she said to herself. 'They must be sold.'

To her surprise, after trying on the hats at varying angles, each lady decided to buy one! Grandmother was fully aware that the few pennies she charged for the hats were well below market price. But, with her earthly philosophy, two sales in one day seemed a good beginning.

From then on, Grandmother went about the neighbourhood selling more hats. For those friends and neighbours who couldn't quite manage to come up with the asking price, she would arrange for them to pay a little each week until the bill was paid in full.

After checking her tin money box, hidden above the mantelpiece, which was now gradually filling up with shillings, sixpences and pennies, Grandmother felt a satisfaction unknown before. Her perseverance in obtaining extra money was finally beginning to pay off. She realized that ladies from all walks of life liked wearing large picturesque, Victorian hats, which gave them an added pride and, perhaps, a feeling of well-being.

Grandmother's hats were beautifully made, with perfect stitching, each one an original; no two alike. Her next venture was to open up a millinery shop close to home. Extra money now coming in would allow her not only to purchase bigger and better varieties of fabrics, but also to indulge in the odd luxury or two. Life for the Ashbys was definitely on the upward trend; the future looking brighter. And all due to Grandmother's foresight and hard work – and to her daughters' nimble fingers.

As her daughters became older, and were growing into beautiful young women with wasp-like waists and shoulder-length hair, an underlying situation involving an over-attentive father was beginning to rear itself. Sensing what was happening, Grandmother decided to take matters into her own hands. Forever protective, and having reared six of her girls practically alone, she was not about to allow anything or anyone to take advantage of them at this stage, and promptly nipped in the bud what could have become a family scandal.

Knowing that given half a chance, and with the takings of the millinery shop in his pocket, Grandfather would quench his thirst on his way home at the local pub, thinking he'd earned this right as "breadwinner", Grandmother decided to send two of her girls on the errand to ensure the pennies and sixpences arrived safely home, and were put into her tin money box.

On every street corner in the East End of London you will find a pub; the temptation to call in for a "quickie" is characteristic of those charismatic Londoners, so full of cheeky humour, who delight in social gossip while swilling down a beer or two. Sometimes this occurred much to the chagrin of their families who were struggling to put food on the table, and hold body and soul together. Survival was by no means an easy task when work for some men was hard to come by.

The idea of Grandfather helping himself to the money from the sale of the hats which required hours of labour and skill in the selling of them, was not in Grandmother's plans to stabilize an on-going business. Forever conscious life had more to offer, and fully aware her husband's wage would never be enough to achieve her goals, she increased the number of new hats and from the sale of these, with the extra money, opened up a second-hand clothing shop, trading in used garments and any odd bits and pieces of china or glassware she could lay her hands on that might be of value. In an old snapshot, her two young sons proudly stand outside the shop window, with the name "Ashby" emblazoned above the front door.

The millinery shop continued to thrive, as did the second-hand clothing shop. So much so that Grandmother then opened up a third business, an antique shop, to her immense pride and joy. It's unimaginable to think that many years later I would be sitting in one of her antique chairs, when visiting a first cousin living in Sussex. If she was proud then, it certainly was a proud moment for me. Her hard work and perseverance in not only rearing eight children on a pitiful wage, and running successful businesses, showed Grandmother to be made of stern stuff, unwilling to give up until she reached her goal for a better life for her family, come what may.

My great-grandfather realized from the start his son-in-law would never amount to much in life, and that the responsibilities of his family would bear heavily on the shoulders of his youngest daughter. John and Mary Turner would have been proud of their daughter knowing how successful she had become, and without any help from either one of them.

Grandmother was indeed a very remarkable person. Her faith in Christian beliefs gave her the courage when struggling throughout her child-bearing years, and enabled her to finally reach the light at the end of the tunnel. I have often wondered if Grandfather ever appreciated what she did for his family. Of course, I'll never know. The one question uppermost, is why did he take note of other women when he had a wife who was not only beautiful, but also a loving, caring mother?

Perhaps in order to clear his conscience, as a final act of kindness, Grandfather Ashby purchased a private grave in Forest Hill, London, cemetery at a cost of ten pounds, sixteen shilling and sixpence to bury Grandmother, when she passed away in 1944.

According to my brother Rowland, who met Grandmother when a lad of thirteen, she was a typical, homely-type grandmother who wore her hair in a neat bun at the back of her head, tied with a black velvet ribbon. Over her dress, she wore a white, crisply-starched apron. She was perfection, to the end.

As my aunts became of age and left school, in order to allay her fears of indiscretion, Grandmother placed them in what she thought were houses of reputable employers, to work as domestic servants.

A picture of Aunt Ada, with large brown eyes, her top lip slightly curled, shows her face with a look of pain on it. She is sitting with a baby on her lap, and wearing a large Victorian hat.

Aunt Lillian Mary married at twenty-three years of age and became a widow five years later. She remarried, to a man named Patrick O'Connor.

In October 1927, she passed away in Camberwell, London, at thirty-six years of age.

Aunt Rose Eveline passed away at Guy's Hospital in London, March 1901, at the age of five.

Aunt Nellie married William Mansfield Middleton in 1917, at twenty-one years of age. It was a double wedding with Janet Mansfield Hilton and Walter Frederick Phillips. A fun-loving person who lived life to the full, Aunt Nellie passed away in 1987.

The photographs I have of Aunt Marie in 1917, aged seventeen and a half years, shows her with long brown, curly hair. Her large eyes are penetrating; she is beautiful, with a beguiling smile. In a later photograph although still as beautiful, there is a look of sadness on her face. Over soft curls, she wears a large hat. She emigrated to Australia, where she passed away in 1973, leaving behind one daughter.

Of my five aunts, Nellie and Marie appealed to me the most. It is Marie's beauty that draws me to her. With Nellie, every photograph shows her laughing, full of vigour, enjoying the moment. And, of course, wearing hats. Aunt Nellie and my mother were the closest of friends. That she knew all of her sister's secrets, I have no doubts whatsoever.

Uncle Ernest married a young girl named Phyllis in 1933. During World War Two, he became an officer in the Royal Army Medical Corps. In February 1989, he passed away in Lincolnshire. His wife died shortly thereafter.

In 1948 Uncle Robert married Rose Emily Thurley. Both have now passed on.

MOTHER'S FIRST MARRIAGE

Like her sisters, my mother Caroline Ashby was a good-looking woman. Of medium height, with brown eyes and long, curly hair, she lived life to the full! Having a shapely pair of legs, she seized every opportunity to go to all the dancehalls in London – where she would show off her legs in such a way that she attracted men like moths to a candle, which eventually caused her downfall.

When in her teens, she entered a dancehall competition, winning first prize. Not only possessing attractive legs, she also had an exceptional voice, and Mother's passion for music found her singing whenever the mood took her, cheering up her nearest and dearest. Like other young people of her generation, she tended to enjoy the good things in life – music taking priority above all else.

Her first serious love affair was with a young Roman Catholic Italian, named Antonio Capolongo, whom she married at the age of twenty-one on January 4, 1910. The wedding vows were taken in the Church of Our Lady and St. Frederick, Limehouse, Stepney, in the East End of London. Antonio was also twenty-one years of age.

The history of the Limehouse mission, also known as the Gunboat Church, goes back to 1881 when a house was acquired in the long, unsightly Commercial Road. The dining-room served as a chapel until such time as the humble church and its schools were built for the numerous Catholic children of the district.

Father Frederick Maples, a former member of the community of the London Oratory, dedicated the new church at Limehouse under the invocation of Our Lady Immaculate. Because of his particular devotion to St. Frederick, his church then became known as Our Lady and St. Frederick.

Many years later, still located on Commercial Road, the church is called our Lady Immaculate Limehouse. Such was Father Maples's devotion that he bore practically the whole financial burden of the new parish, until he relinquished the charge at the end of 1885.

Little is known about Antonio Capolongo, other than he was a Master Fruiterer living with his parents at 148 Ben Johnson Road, Mile End, London. His father, also named Antonio, was an Ice Cream Vendor. His type of business was much in vogue when Italians migrated to England in the late 1800s, and settled into the various boroughs of London. They were noticeable in the London markets where they served from fruit stalls and opened up ice cream parlours, which provided them with a lucrative living. But it was hard work for many who found it difficult to get space at the market, as stalls were in great demand. Over the years, as more and more vendors populated the areas, space became a serious problem for those fruit traders anxious to find what was then known as a "pitch".

For as long as I can remember, London, the East End in particular, boasted the best outdoor markets and fruit stalls, where the bartering for goods became a recognized ritual. To watch the barrow boys go about their business was a scene you couldn't forget. Such roughish characters, they wheeled and dealed their wares; the entertainment they performed was as good, if not better, than going to one of the old music halls familiar to London in the early 1920s.

On September 13, 1911 Caroline gave birth to a baby girl at Walworth, London, whom the parents christened Marie. The young child was baptized in the Catholic Church of the English Martyrs, when just three weeks old.

Sadly, Caroline's marriage to Antonio was short-lived after their daughter developed bronchial-pneumonia and was admitted into Queen Mary's Hospital at Carshalton in the County of Surrey, where she died when just sixteen months of age. When this tragedy occurred, nothing else mattered to my mother. With the loss of her child she slowly drifted further and further away from her husband, finally moving back to London in order to pick up the pieces of her life.

After many years of extensive and non-productive record searching for the whereabouts of Antonio Capolongo, we can only surmise he may have returned to Italy, possibly the place of his birth, prior to the outbreak of World War One in 1914. Alternatively, he could have rejoined his family who were still living in London. However, for him to have remained with his parents is questionable in view of the fact he is not listed in any of the records in England, including the death indexes held at St. Catherine's House in London.

His disappearance from the time of his daughter's death remains a mystery. Could he have joined the British Forces in the 1914 war, and been killed? There are no records to this effect. Antonio would have had to be a British subject for him to enter any of the armed forces – which, that being the case, would confirm he was born in England and not Italy.

Another puzzling question: did Antonio and Caroline ever divorce? With Antonia being a Roman Catholic, it would seem highly unlikely. Divorces in the nineteenth and early twentieth century were not a common occurrence, and anyone involved in this type of court case was frowned upon by the establishment, regardless of one's position in life. All divorces were considered a public scandal and both parties, whether guilty or innocent, carried with them the stigma of being divorced, for life. Such were the dominant laws and social ruling in Britain.

With their marriage floundering, a husband and wife would normally remain together, perhaps if only to save face, or "for the sake of the children". The likelihood here, is that Antonio, being a Catholic, would never have consented to a divorce. On the other hand, did Caroline wait until the normal three years had elapsed before entering into a second marriage, prior to her first marriage being annulled?

I made a request to the Principal Registry of the Family Division, Somerset House, Strand, London, for a search of the central index of divorce Decree Absolute for the years 1910 to 1919 inclusive. It was certified that no trace could be found of a Decree Absolute relating to Antonio and Caroline Capolongo. This record was dated January 1944.

Following up on this, an inquiry was made to the Census, Office of Populations, at St. Catherine's House in February 1995, and where I was referred to the Office of Population, Census and Surveys, Farnham, Surrey. There, staff advised me that records are held in strict confidence for a period of 100 years by virtue of an instrument under the 1958 *Public Records Act*, under a concession originally announced in Parliament in 1972.

The Register General of the OPCS may consider a concession, allowing certain information from the 1911 Census to be released, but only for the purpose of establishing a legal settlement such as an inheritance. All my other efforts to trace the occupants of 107 Hellena House, Borden Row, Newington, where Antonio and Caroline Capolongo lived, have proved futile.

MOTHER'S SECOND MARRIAGE

Never one to stay idle for long, my mother decided to become a stewardess on one of the passenger liners sailing from Southampton, England, to Sydney, Australia. While Caroline's other sisters were already married, her sister Marie remained unwed in 1913 and had already undertaken one or two of these journeys between the two countries. Knowing my mother was still grieving over the loss of her baby (also named Marie), Aunt Marie encouraged her sister to join her on the next available voyage, thinking it would do her good to be in new surroundings and see new faces. With their plans in place, the sisters became inseparable, making sure that when they signed on a ship, they would remain together. Unfortunately, with England on the brink of World War One in 1914, these pleasurable journeys came to an abrupt end.

It was somewhere in London that my mother, at twenty-seven years of age, met a handsome fellow in the Royal Navy named Edward Rutley Pocock Marshall. Edward was born in 1884 at Lydd in the County of Kent, and came from down-to-earth people who lived all their lives in a farming community. His father Edward Rutley Marshall (born 1864), and his father before him, Alfred Leaver Marshall (born 1821), never stepped far from their homes other than to work in the fields of Eastern Kent, and prided themselves on maintaining and supporting their families.

My grandfather Edward Rutley Marshall looked a typical farmer, sporting a huge walrus mustache. Such was his pride in the name "Rutley", he expected every male member of his family to be thus christened with his middle name. It would cause him to become rather grumpy if relatives didn't comply to his wishes.

Like many of his ilk who appeared to be simple, law-abiding farmers, he was given to smuggling contraband brought in by ships that lay off the coast at night. As with many of their co-conspirators operating around the south coast of England, the smugglers made a mockery of authority. The risk of being caught red-handed and prosecuted was of no concern to the culprits, who frequently ran trips between the channel ports of France and England for supplies of illegal goods.

Using a system of underground tunnels from the beaches, the smugglers managed to sneak ashore the contraband, such as barrels of rum and tobacco, under the very noses of custom officials. Sometimes, when being offered a drink by a well-wisher, little did the official realize the very rum he was drinking was illegal. To the rum runners, stolen goods whet the appetite, making these more palatable to the taste buds. Also, where was the fun to life if a little excitement wasn't thrown in, to cause a heart flutter or two? Leading simple, country lives within the farming community, each man found that with this type of skulduggery going on around him, the adrenalin flowed to such a pitch it achieved not only a feeling of euphoria, but also an excitement he'd never before experienced. To give it all up by being caught red-handed, was not what any smuggler had in mind.

When trips were made across the channel, the smugglers were a well-organized gang with every man depending on the other for all plans to work. None of these darkly-held secrets were ever divulged to their womenfolk for fear that, if idle gossip spread within the community, the outcome could be disastrous. Incomes would be lost and the culprits, when caught, would be sent to prison for a lengthy period of time. For this, and other reasons, silence was golden at all cost. Little did they realize, in that particular parish, the leader of the smugglers was indeed the holy vicar himself.

Edward Rutley Marshall had two wives during his lifetime. He was happily married to eighteen-year-old Mary Pocock in 1885. After giving birth to three sons (Edward being the eldest), followed by three daughters, Mary passed away at the age of thirty-one. His second marriage was to a

Sarah Wood and from this marriage, he had three daughters. Living a life with both comforts and secret adventure, Edward Rutley Marshall passed away in 1953 at ninety years of age, and was buried in the cemetery at All Saints Church, Lydd, Kent.

One of his well-known characteristics shows he was a gentle man, with a big heart. Throughout his life, he religiously carried with him a small penknife and, whenever a child went to him, he would pick an apple off the tree and with a precise stroke of the penknife, cut a section out of the apple and hand it to the child.

Watching the child smile when accepting the slice of apple, he would give a wide smile back and affectionately pat the child on the top of the head. This simple deed of love gave him great joy. He adored his family and, despite being a bit of a rascal where the law was concerned, he was a loving father and a good provider. When his eldest son Edward joined the Navy and made a name for himself, the old man knew of no greater pride. It was a though he himself had been lifted to great heights.

In 1902, young Edward signed on with the Royal Navy as Boy Second Class. He was five-foot, seven-inches tall, with light blue eyes, light brown hair and fair complexion. He was eighteen years old. His steady rise through the ranks from commencement of service, saw him go from Boy First Class, to Chief Petty Officer by 1915. He served with distinction on many of His Majesty's ships, from frigates to cruisers. Naval records show him to be of excellent character, and superior in efficiency.

Shore leave could not come soon enough for Edward, who wasted little time travelling to London to meet my mother on every occasion. As weeks went by, Caroline knew she was madly in love with this strikingly-handsome man and wanted more than anything to marry him. Knowing that, with World War One in full progress, Edward could be forced overseas at any moment, they decided to get married in October 1915, at St. Matthias Church in the Parish of Islington, London. Their honeymoon, however, was to be short-lived – Edward received orders from Naval authorities to return to his base, immediately.

With all leave cancelled, his ship sailed to the Port of Salonika in Greece. During the First World War, the Allies landed here in 1915, using the city as a base for the Salonika campaigns, which culminated in the 1918 defeat of the German and Bulgarian divisions in the Balkans. Following the cessation of hostilities, the Royal Navy took over as guardians of the Dardanelles, to keep the passage open for ships of all nations.

With the news that her newly-wed husband was on a two-year engagement at the Naval base in Salonika and would not be home before early 1918, my mother decided to seek work as a Royal Auxiliary nurse while Britain and the Allies were still at war. Perhaps her thoughts were, if she kept busy by helping nurse the wounded, it would take her mind off the separation until her husband returned home to England. Many women were recruited as R.A. nurses during the war, taking on menial tasks so that those who were fully qualified in the medical profession were able to give more care and attention to the badly wounded.

When Edward finally ended his service in Salonika in 1918 and went on his first shore leave, he was reunited with my mother who by then had returned to the swing of things, in London.

With the end of hostilities on November 11, 1918, everyone who had served their country was of the opinion it had been "a war to end all wars". Sadly, this was not to be the case.

A few months after Edward's return, my mother found herself pregnant and in January 1919 she gave birth to her second child, a son named Rowland, who was born at 182 Westmoreland Road, Walworth, London. This was in the same institution in which her first child, Marie, was born.

In 1919 Edward once again was travelling the high seas, and it was during this period that the ship's company had on board a special member of the Royal Family. It was Edward VIII, Prince of Wales, who left Portsmouth for Canada aboard *HMS Renown* on August 5, 1919, arriving at Conception Bay, Newfoundland, on August 11. From Newfoundland the light cruiser *HMS Dragon* conveyed the Prince to Saint John, the capital of New Brunswick. Here he made his first landing on Canadian soil on August 15. Throughout August, September and October, the Prince of Wales' schedule took him to many places in Canada, including Toronto, where he received a tumultuous welcome by the crowds.

To commemorate his visit to Toronto, a photograph was taken of the ship's company of *HMS Dragon* in front of the City Hall, in the presence of Toronto's Mayor and other dignitaries. My father is in that photograph.

During this period, having to care for a small baby, my mother found her lifestyle somewhat curtailed. She loved music, dancing, and recognized the fact that child-rearing was not one of her talents. This tiny child suddenly found himself picked up into the arms of a total stranger, also a sailor, though of little rank, with whom my mother had become secretly involved. Her relationship with this man would be her worst mistake, and one she would live to regret for the rest of her life. This clandestine affair brought my mother to her knees, such was the influence of this sailor who pursued her relentlessly.

MOTHER'S THIRD MARRIAGE

John Brandon was born 1890 in Dublin, Ireland, of Irish parentage. Five-feet, three-inches tall, with brown hair and grey eyes, he boasted a scar on the centre of his forehead and one on his right forearm. He joined the Royal Navy in Belfast on July 4, 1910, on a twelve-year engagement, as a Stoker II Class.

Brandon served overseas on destroyers and cruisers from his Port Division in Portsmouth, Hampshire, between the years 1910 to July 1922 when he was released ashore, the period of his continuous service having expired. He then joined the Royal Fleet Reserve October 1924, based at Portsmouth and was discharged in 1932.

The Union Jack Club in Waterloo Road, London, opened its doors to all servicemen, providing them with dormitory lodging while on leave. Along with other comings and goings at this well-known establishment, many sailors were known to have spent their honeymoon at the club, perhaps having met their future wives while in London.

On December 17, 1919, John Brandon a thirty-one-year-old bachelor, married Caroline Florence Hinks, purportedly a spinster of the same age. If the information given to the Registrar at the time of his marriage was correct, it would indicate he was born in 1888 and not 1890, as shown on his Naval records. This wouldn't be the only dubious information on the marriage certificate.

Brandon, a Stoker in His Majesty's Navy, gave his address on the marriage certificate as the Union Jack Club, Waterloo Road. His father, John Brandon (deceased) was a Ship's Rigger Foreman. Caroline Florence Hinks described herself as a Wardrobe Dealer who lived at 54

Bath Terrace, Union Road. Her father, Joseph Hinks (deceased), was listed as a General Dealer. It may be co-incidental, but worthy of note, that fathers of both bride and groom were listed as deceased.

Caroline Florence Hinks, a spinster when she married Brandon in The Register Office in the District of Southwark, East End of London, appeared to be the mother of an eleven-month-old boy, but no record can be found to substantiate this birth. On the other hand, Caroline Marshall, the wife of Edward Rutley Pocock Marshall, also had a boy of the same age, born 1919, whose birth is recorded at St. Catherine's House, London, under the name of Rowland Charles Marshall.

In July 1921, Caroline Florence (Hinks) Brandon gave birth to a daughter named Margaret in Kennington, London. In the birth record of this happy event, Brandon, now sporting three stripes on his sleeve, classified himself as a First Class Stoker. His address was given as 25 Lambeth Square, London.

On November 6, 1921 John and Caroline took a small boy named Ronald Charles Brandon, then nearly three years old, to St. George's Cathedral in Southwark where he was baptized into the Catholic faith by the Reverend John Farrell. After this Christian deed was done, the young boy was put out of the way, into a Catholic convent in the County of Sussex, December 1921.

Brandon and his wife were then free to look after their baby, Margaret, without the burden of rearing another child, thus enabling them to indulge in other pleasurable pursuits.

Decades later, when I made an inquiry to the Mother Generalate of the convent in Sussex for details of Ronald Charles Brandon, in her reply she stated: 'Charles Brandon, son of John and Caroline. Parents came from Dublin, Ireland.'

She went on to give his date of birth as January 1919, and where he was baptized.

Strangely enough, in the convent's records which I examined a few years ago, there appears to be no entry of when Ronald Charles Brandon made his First Communion, or Confirmation, or when he left the convent. These omissions of details or missing details are extremely odd, considering that looking after the many thousands of children in their care, the Catholic schools and convent's main aim was to ensure all souls were saved – thereby Communion and Confirmation were essential teachings to the upbringing of Catholic children. It is hardly feasible to assume that young Ronald Charles was exempt from taking these ritual practices of the church, but the question is, why were the details of his religion never recorded? Ronald Charles Brandon is not even listed as having been entered into the convent, in the first place.

Taking the young child by the hand, an elderly gentleman whose name is not recorded in the register, apparently took him to the convent and handed him over to one of the nuns, to be educated. There is no record of who paid for his upkeep over the next ten years. It was the responsibility of either the parents or a guardian to pay the required fees before any child was allowed entry into the convent. To this day, the child's benefactor remains a mystery.

Thinking there might possibly be a link with the Southwark Diocese, whose offices are at Purley in the County of Surrey, England, I made an appointment in 1993 to see the Diocese's Archivist, Mr. Lyons. Between us we thoroughly searched through the heavy volumes of numerous old records of children who were placed in Catholic homes during the early 1920s, but no trace could be found of this three-year-old boy, Ronald Charles Brandon, who was admitted into a convent in 1921. No record could be found either to show if the Southwark Diocese had accepted responsibility for the child's upkeep. It is clear this boy did not go through the normal channels of the Catholic Children's Rescue Society, that took in thousands of children from poverty-stricken areas of London. These children were fed and clothed from the Society's funds, most of which coming from various Union Boards and public donations.

A mystery surrounding this vulnerable child came to light when he was told at thirteen years of age by the Mother Superior, 'Your mother wants you to go home now, Ronald.'

The shock when hearing this piece of news left him speechless! There had been no contact with his parents since the day he entered the convent. He considered himself an orphan and had always been told so.

Today, genealogists are well aware that records – specifically those held by religious organisations – leave much to be desired as far as keeping accurate details of children who were put under their care. The majority of these care-givers were only concerned with the saving of a child's soul – nothing more, nothing less – and, if possible, generating revenues and expanding the enterprises of the Church. Record-keeping was not important to them. Thus, when in later years these same children were researching family history, they found it not only to be a daunting task but many were to realize the name they were known under as a child, was not their true name. Obtaining a birth certificate was the only way to prove their identity.

The ignorance of those people wearing the cloth showed in their couldn't-care-less attitude. When questioned by curious family seekers, they told them over and over again: 'that was the way things were done in those days, so – let sleeping dogs lie. What you don't know, you won't miss.'

It wasn't the answer children wanted to hear, but their questions continued to fall on deaf ears. Children borne out of wedlock carried a heavy burden within, and were constantly reminded by their care-givers, 'The sins of the parents shall be visited on the children.'

Much was the fear in every child when hearing this frightening expression, which left them wondering if they themselves had done something so dreadfully bad, for this was God's way of punishing them.

All efforts to trace birth records or a possible divorce in the name of John Brandon and Caroline Florence Hinks have proven futile to this day. Because of a 1922 fire in Ireland, all relevant documents on births, marriages and deaths were destroyed. Invaluable, historical information literally went up in smoke. The work to dig up ancestral history is formidable in itself, but with so many records burnt in the 1922 fire, the task of finding the smallest piece of information on anyone in Ireland in the 1800s, is practically impossible. A few of the churches in Ireland have some parish records but, unless one knows the area or religious denominations relating to an ancestor, searching becomes futile.

Correspondence going back and forth for information on John Brandon since 1992 to the Hibernian Research Company, Dun Laoghaire Rathdown Heritage Project and the Irish Genealogical Research Society has proved unsuccessful. It's as though this man never existed, and has simply disappeared without trace.

According to the birth register held at the Greater London Record Office and Library, 40 Northampton Road, London, Caroline Florence Brandon (née Hinks) gave birth to a son named William at the Lambeth Hospital, in the Sub-District of Kennington, in February 1924. It was the same hospital in which she had given birth to her daughter Margaret three years before.

AN AWKWARD HOMECOMING

In the summer of 1924, having completed his final duty on *HMS Pembroke* from November 9, 1921 to June 21, 1924, Chief Petty Officer Marshall terminated his service with the Royal Navy. Of good character, he had been awarded three Good Conduct Medals: in 1906, 1910 and 1915. In 1917 he also received another medal, awarded for Long Service and Good Conduct.

A few weeks after arriving home to his wife, now living at 72 Westminster Bridge Road, London, he noticed a gradual change in Caroline's usual happy-go-lucky mood. Her behaviour appeared far from normal and he sensed something was very wrong – but what, he had yet to put a finger on it. Constantly in a state of nervousness, as though dreading ghosts of the past to suddenly descend upon her, she was not the happy woman whom he had married.

Now receiving a Naval pension, work did not seem an important factor to Edward. His main concern was to settle down with his wife after many long separations while serving abroad. He wanted to make up for the little time he'd spent with her throughout their nine years of marriage, but realized the transition from Navy life to civvy life would not be an easy one.

By December 1924, Caroline found herself once again to be pregnant. Despite the fact her real husband was the father of her child, she did not bargain for what was about to happen. When it did, her life was ruined to the point of despair, and she would face endless misery and poverty never before experienced.

During the intervening weeks of taking up civilian life, Edward somehow discovered his wife had committed adultery while he was away at sea, and was utterly taken aback by what he had heard. Never suspecting for a moment she had been disloyal to him, he'd had every confidence of receiving a warm welcome home when he returned to her in London. He looked forward, more than anything, to a happy life ahead.

The news, that Caroline had given birth to two other children during the time her husband was away, shocked him to the point of total disbelief and caused him to wonder: 'how can this happen to me?'

His wife, now six months pregnant with his child, was told by Edward in no uncertain manner that he was filing for a divorce, on the grounds of adultery.

The trauma of this unfortunate affair rested squarely on Caroline's shoulders; she would live to regret her improprieties. Instead of waiting for her husband to return home from overseas, she had chosen to cavort around in the arms of another man, a sailor describing himself as a First Class Stoker. Caroline was besotted by this man of dubious character with whom she had become involved in a scandalous love affair, resulting in the birth of her two children. There was the illegal marriage. Did Edward ever find out the name of her children's father – John Brandon?

It is impossible to determine whose name was cited as co-respondent in the divorce papers, due to the Case File number being lost. A fair guess, I feel sure, would point to the Stoker, with whom mother had had the lengthy elicit affair, and who had disappeared from the scene by the time Edward returned home in 1924.

In the High Court of Justice in London on June 22, 1925, an application for divorce was entered by Edward. On January 18, 1926, the decree nisi was made absolute, dissolving the marriage solemnized on October 13, 1915 between Edward Rutley Pocock Marshall and Caroline Marshall (née Ashby).

Caroline was now heavily pregnant, and totally alone, except for her parents who still lived at Peckham Rye, London, and whom she visited from time to time. Her ex-husband, however, did not deem it his responsibility to provide her with an allowance. He was no longer interested in the mother of his son and impending child, and washed his hands of her – and them – forever.

A little girl she named Caroline was born September 1925, in Walworth, London, and baptized at the local Catholic Church of the English Martyrs. The birth certificate records the name of Edward Rutley Pocock Marshall as the father, formerly Chief Petty Officer of His Majesty's Navy.

After the birth of her child, my mother's life tells a tragic story of the suffering she endured, and of the appalling conditions under which she was forced to live.

Angus Baxter and his contact with the Head Archivist of the Greater London Record Office were able to extract from their records certain chronological details outlining the desperate events of my mother's life. She was recorded as having been in and out of the workhouse, with no means to support herself or her child, from the time I was born. The question here is, 'where were her other two children – Margaret and William, apparently fathered by John Brandon – during these intervening months, and under whose care?'

Although adamant to face the truth about my birth and early life, the information I was about to receive left me with the feeling that I wasn't going to like all that would be uncovered. But I knew I would never rest until all the sordid details were revealed.

Most of us realize truth always hurts, it's never the healer. Sadly, truth was not one of my mother's virtues.

For the child, hiding a stigma, while an easy way out, does not unburden one's conscience. Somehow, it will surface, only to haunt you again and again into the depths of your soul, making you more determined than ever to find out just exactly who you are.

The records Angus Baxter and his associate located show that Caroline Marshall (née Ashby) born 1888, age given as thirty-seven, was admitted to the Institution in Walworth, September 21, 1925 from 72 Westminster Bridge Road, London. She was listed as married and her occupation was "Wardrobe Dealer". The Institution provided the minimal nursing care for births by destitute women.

It is interesting to note that when Caroline Florence Hinks married

John Brandon in December 1919, she gave her occupation as Wardrobe Dealer.

Caroline gave her religious creed as Church of England. Her nearest relative was listed as her mother, Elizabeth Ashby, 115 Albany Flats. Caroline's daughter was born on September 25, and her religious creed was given as Roman Catholic. Both were discharged at the request of the mother on October 17, 1925.

They were re-admitted on November 28, 1925. Caroline gave her nearest relative this time as her husband, but no name or address. Mother and child were discharged on January 30, 1926, only to be re-admitted as homeless on February 2, discharged February 3, and re-admitted February 8.

Daughter Caroline's creed is again given as Roman Catholic, and her mother as Church of England. Both were discharged to the Southwark Board of Guardians' Hospital at East Dulwich Grove, London, on March 29, 1926 and re-admitted to the institution from there on April 3, to be discharged June 10.

On August 30, 1926 Caroline and her daughter were again admitted and discharged on September 13, 1926. There were no further entries for mother and daughter until August 19, 1927. On that date they were admitted, Caroline had another child with her named Elizabeth born March 1927, also Roman Catholic. They were homeless. Caroline's occupation was now given as a kitchen hand. Her marital status as "M & D" (married and divorced).

Elizabeth was discharged to the Southwark Hospital on August 20, 1927. Mother and daughter Caroline were discharged on September 8. On September 9, 1927, baby Caroline of Roman Catholic faith was admitted from Carter Street Police. She had been deserted.

A Justice's Order was issued in the County of Kent, April 1928, and approved by the court to have Mother's four children – Margaret, William, Caroline and Elizabeth – removed from the Southwark Union, who at that time were caring for the children. Because the Southwark Union's charges were considered excessive, new caregivers would be found, with the Canterbury Guardians willing to maintain the three older children at a nominal fee of seventeen shillings and sixpence each per week, and the youngest one at twelve shillings and sixpence per week. The three girls would remain in one institution, the boy in another.

There was no mention of Rowland, Mother's first son, in the court order. This puzzled me as all Mother's other children were taken into account. The only reason I could come up with was that, perhaps, due to him being known as Brandon and hidden away in a convent at Littlehampton, Sussex, in 1921, the court was unaware of his existence; therefore they did not connect him to the Marshall children.

Such were the unfortunate events following the unhappy homecoming of my father, whom I never had the privilege to meet.

ANOTHER MARRIAGE FOR FATHER

While my mother's relationship with men left much to be desired, I also suspect my father didn't exactly have a clean record, either. The old saying, "a sailor has a girl in every port", makes me feel this might have been the case where a particular woman was concerned who lived in Plymouth, Devon. Plymouth is an old established Naval base in the South of England, and my father had been stationed there. It would seem natural for him to meet the local ladies at dances, held at the service clubs.

On January 18, 1926, my father's divorce became absolute, dissolving his marriage to my mother. No longer living in London, he took up residence at Rochester, Kent, in the South East of England.

Rochester is not only a beautiful city, but an historic one. Its roots go back to Roman times; it has a fine Norman Castle, one of the oldest cathedrals in England and an excellent example of a Victorian High Street. Situated on the River Medway, it has long been an important strategic river crossing on the road from London to Canterbury and Dover. The importance of the river crossing reached a peak in Norman times when the castle was constructed and the City was granted its first Royal Charter. The river continued to be important until modern times because of the Naval dockyard at nearby Chatham.

In November 1926, my father married for the second time to Sarah Ring at The Parish Church in Rochester. He was forty-two years of age, having legally divorced from his former wife Caroline Marshall (née Ashby) some ten months previous. Sarah was thirty-seven years old, a widow, whose family came from Plymouth. She was a good-looking woman with fair hair, five-feet, eight-inches tall, and considered to be an excellent housekeeper.

Listening to family members' comments about her, it seems Sarah was a somewhat overpowering woman, with a strong character, who had a tendency to be rather bossy. Apparently, not too many of Edward's family in Kent were drawn to her, in particular his eldest sister, Elizabeth. Jim Cobley, a relative living at Lydd, confirmed these sentiments, noting that no one appeared comfortable in the company of Aunt Sarah.

With Father having been stationed at the Naval base in Plymouth, there is every possibility this is where the two of them met. Not long after they were married in 1926, my father purchased a house on Arthur Road in Rochester, Kent. His family in Lydd would come and visit them from time to time, staying for short holidays.

After eight years in civilian life, for whatever the reason, Edward decided to rejoin the Navy on January 9, 1934. At the time, he was fifty years of age. His Naval base now being at Chatham, Kent, meant he was stationed closer to home. How Sarah felt about this turn of events, is hard to imagine. She was, after all, a woman with a strong mind, but perhaps she doted on him and gave way to his decision to re-enlist in the Navy. His last two months of service were at his old shore base, *HMS Pembroke*, and on September 28, 1939 his career in the Navy was finally over. He had served his king and country for twenty-seven years, at home and abroad.

Upon checking his Navy records through the co-operation of the Ministry of Defence at Hayes in the County of Middlesex, who hold records of all servicemen, I was surprised to note 'No next-of-kin' recorded. I found this very strange because, initially, when he first joined the Navy as a boy his father Edward Rutley Marshall was still living, though not with his biological mother. Perhaps he didn't get on too well with his step-mother, Sarah Wood, and this may have caused him to refrain from giving the authorities his family details.

When I questioned this oversight with Angus Baxter, his comment was one of surprise: 'It must be borne in mind that the information he gave about his name and age must be accurate, because a Naval rating would have to provide the certificates as proof of age, marriage, next-of-kin, and family to his superior officer,' said Angus. 'Accurate information would be required for his rate of pay, pension on discharge, and death benefits for his family if he was killed in action.'

After my father was discharged ashore from the Royal Navy, he returned to Chatham and worked in the dockyard until reaching retirement age. At seventy-three years of age, he passed away on December 31, 1957 and was cremated at Churt in the County of Kent.

On a trip to England in 1988, I visited not only his old house on Arthur Road, but the Crematorium at Churt. I was told by a staff member, who checked the records, that my father's ashes were scattered around an old oak tree, where daffodils grow in abundance. His name is in the Remembrance Book, showing the date he died. The gardens are meticulously kept, with lush-green lawns, and colourful shrubs everywhere. I'm sure he would have been happy to know Sarah's choice for his eternal rest, was in the Garden of Remembrance.

During this particular visit my own thoughts turned to sadness as I stood and gazed at the ground where he is buried. Looking back on life, I wondered if the fates might have been kinder to me had this man, who was my true father, chosen to recognize me as his daughter.

Visiting the house in Rochester where he had once lived, a young couple now in possession of the property were delighted to show me around after I explained to them that my father had lived there some years ago. I did not, of course, tell them the very bedroom in which they now sleep, is where he had passed away.

They pointed out to me the numerous renovations they had made since buying the property. I noticed the paintwork throughout was fresh and colourful. Looking out from the kitchen window, into the garden below, an old Victorian high-brick wall is built around it, over which hang masses of coloured roses. The peaceful setting must have given Edward and Sarah a feeling of "belonging". It was a beautiful garden.

Sarah didn't remain long in the house on Arthur Road after her husband's death. Once his Will was settled she moved back to Plymouth in Devon, to be with her family. A short time later, she passed away. She was in her seventies. Sarah had no children.

Through a neighbour who lived close to my father, I was able to find out the address in Plymouth where Sarah's two nieces still live. I wrote to them and asked if they had any photographs of my father. By return mail they enclosed three pictures of him which I was delighted to receive. In one picture he looks tall, upright, wearing a good suit of clothing and a hat. The place looks like Plymouth as I knew it years ago. Walking beside him is a black Labrador dog. Another photo shows him quite young-looking, sitting on a chair, and holding a small child on his left knee. Whose child, I wonder? The third picture is of him, Sarah, and her two nieces, sitting in deck chairs.

Another photograph taken in Rochester, given to me by a first cousin from Lydd, shows my father looking a lot older. He is standing next to Sarah, his eldest sister Elizabeth and her son Roland, with his two young boys. In the photo, Sarah is still good-looking. My father has a benign smile on his face. He looks to be a happy, gentle man. Would I have liked to know, or have met him? Without question, yes, as I think our relationship could have been quite special.

My mother, who caused him so much pain when charting her own course and leaving him emotionally floundering on the rocks, so to speak, must have been reason enough for him to ignore his son and daughter. I cannot bring myself to blame him.

Ironically, when my father lived at Rochester, I was living at Petts Wood in the County of Kent, in the mid-1950s, just miles away from him.

Herne Bay, Kent, a seaside resort close to Rochester, is where I spent many happy holiday week-ends. The air is bracing, with strong winds coming in from the ocean; it's a place to pick mussels and cockles, well-known to Londoners, who frequented the stony beaches and enjoyed themselves, away from the hustle and bustle of the big city.

Looking back, this was a sad part of my family's history, but I soon discovered there was more yet to unfold. On the bright side, I'm glad that my father appeared to have found happiness in marriage the second time round.

YET ANOTHER FAMILY FOR MOTHER

lthough Caroline came to use the surname Marshall for her four
children, one can reason this came about because she was still
known by that name. When her daughter Elizabeth was born
in March 1927, she gave the father's name as Edward which, of course,
was far from the truth unless she had known another Edward, but this I
doubt. Knowing Edward Rutley Pocock Marshall had divorced his wife
in January 1926 and was well into his second marriage with Sarah Ring
in 1927, he could not have fathered Elizabeth.

On February 20, 1928, my mother married for the fourth time, to a
forty-two year old bachelor named Percy Edwin Martin. The ceremony
took place in the Register Office at Lambeth, East End of London.
Curiously, the marriage certificate shows Caroline Marshall formerly
Ashby, as a spinster, thirty-nine years of age. It also records: 'the divorced
wife of Edward Rutley Pocock Marshall.'

Caroline's father, Frederick Proudfoot Ashby, is shown as a General
Dealer, another strange footnote in the history of our family.

Once again Caroline found herself six months pregnant when she
entered into her fourth marriage, which perhaps was brought about
because of her condition. It is difficult to comprehend how she could
have fallen for another child when my sister Elizabeth who was born in
March 1927, was just five months old.

'How can this happen?' I thought. 'Where is the logic? And why did
she keep having so many children she could ill-afford?'

Conscious that sex knows no bounds where a lusty, loving woman is concerned, it appears that my mother, who certainly did things her own way, never learned to say 'no' to men who came into 'play'.

In May 1928, she gave birth to a baby boy at the Commercial Road Maternity Hospital, Limehouse, London, named Percy, after his father. Caroline and her husband were then living at Royal Road, Southwark, when their son was born.

In July 1930, a second son named Cecil was born in the same maternity hospital. The family had moved again, this time to Burton Road, Brixton, London. These residences in which they lived were probably flats, with low monthly rents. Perhaps they were moving from one place to another searching for accommodation they could afford and survive, on a bricklayer's wage such as Percy Martin earned.

My mother, now forty-four years of age, had a third son in June 1932, whom she named Kenneth. He was born in Epsom Hospital in the County of Surrey. With her husband and three sons, Caroline moved from London to the countryside of Carshalton, Surrey, where they lived in a house on Merton Road, for several years. This property may have belonged to the local Council, to whom they paid a nominal rent.

Many London families who had worked throughout the summer months during the hop-picking season in various parts of Kent, eventually packed up their families and moved into the outskirts of the country in order to get away from the grime and dirt of London. Most of them were soon able to find work on the many Kentish farms, noted for agriculture and sheep-farming, from which they earned their main source of income.

Percy Martin, who was a keen gardener, grew as many vegetables in the garden as possible to supplement the food bill. But many difficult times lay ahead for him, when trying to support his family. Work in the early '30s was scarce. With such erratic periods of employment he often came home with little, or no money at all. Climatic conditions – when the weather turned extremely cold in the winter, or it rained heavily – often resulted in no work being available for those men who worked outside in the building trade. His many disappointments with earning little wages were, no doubt, the cause of his unhappy facial expression.

He was known as a miserable man, who seldom put a smile on his face, to all good reason, perhaps.

With five hungry mouths to feed, my mother kept herself busy by travelling back and forth to London selling anything she could lay her hands on, from clothing to any odd bits and pieces of minute value, in the hope of getting extra money to add to her husband's meagre wage. When her husband couldn't work, she took full advantage of the bad weather, even looking upon it as a day's outing, and often chanced the opportunity of meeting up with old friends. There were of course times when things got really tough for the family, and she had no alternative but to wrap up her husband's blue serge suit and brown boots and take them to the nearest pawn shop.

The blue serge suit became the butt of many a joke locally, being known as the 'in-d-go-suit'. For example, it would go in on a Tuesday and come out on the following Saturday, when he was paid his weekly wage. This was the only means by which the family could by-pass such hard times when, once again, Mother would trot off to Tooting market in London, around eight o'clock in the evening, before each week-end. Standing with her brown carrier bag at the butcher's stall just at closing time, she would collect the week-end joint of beef and the rest of her shopping, which she purchased at half-price.

While she was gone most of the day, much to his chagrin, her husband took care of the children. Reaching close to fifty years of age, it was not his idea of married bliss. There were, he thought, 'better things to be doing than taking care of small children.' He didn't appreciate it when his wife took off to London, in spite of her efforts to give him financial support, however small. On returning home from her shopping expedition Mother was met with the usual moans and groans from her husband, when he complained bitterly he had no tobacco. Whereupon, Mother would dip into her purse and give him what little she could, from the wage money he'd given her and her few pence earned from trading clothing and other items.

Grandmother Ashby had started up her businesses in much the same way, buying and selling old clothing. By adding additional money to her husband's poor wage, it enabled her to feed her large family and successfully run three shops. My mother obviously had learned from her own mother this secret to survival and any opportunity she had to do so, would be taken with full advantage.

As seen in photographs, Percy Martin was not a handsome man but there was something attractive about him, that made one take a second look. Tall and wiry with black receding hair, he had a military-style clipped moustache. The usual stern expression on his face conveyed that of a strict disciplinarian. While his wife was of a happier disposition who liked to sing and dance, and enjoy the odd stout of beer or two, Martin did not wish to participate in his wife's frivolity. Instead, he chose to sit by the fire, rolling his own cigarettes, filling them with "Nut Brown" tobacco.

He liked his weekly glass of Whitbread's stout, which my mother made sure was there for him every Friday, after work. Often he would come home soaking wet to the skin, exhausted, and in a terrible mood. His family, not wishing to upset him further, kept their distance. In order to try to cheer him up, my mother would sing to him. With her head cocked on one side, she would gaze at him with pity and burst into song, with a rendition of *'Dear face that holds no sweeter smile for me, were you not mine, how dark this world would be,'* hoping to revive some of the lost passion in their lives. This act of Mother's had no affect on him whatsoever. He simply shrugged his shoulders and continued to indulge in miserable silence, deep in his own thoughts, with no wish to participate, or to be happy.

Caroline's favourite songs were those from the music hall days back in the 1920s, which she sang from the heart. Perhaps she sadly realized another mess she had got herself into, with babies to look after, while most mothers of her age were out enjoying themselves, dancing, downing a few gins in the local pub; their children now grown up.

Perhaps memories of her first husband still haunted her, causing her to break into her favourite song: *'Oh, oh, Antonio, he's gone away, he left me all alone.'* It conveyed the sadness she felt when she sang it, thinking no doubt of her first love, and perhaps wondering where her life had gone so terribly wrong. Her husband neither liked music nor understood her reason for wanting to sing. He simply failed to understand her emotions, and would turn away when listening to her voice.

Whatever her failings in life – and she certainly had many which most of us only read about in novels – her first love with Antonio Capolongo was her only true love. Of that I'm sure. Losing her first baby traumatized her, and probably caused her long-term emotional distress and instability. Floundering in all directions, she fell into the arms of any silver-tongued Romeo to whom she took a momentary fancy. Lusty and loving, like many before her and since, she would have a short life and a gay one.

Educated the past ten years in a Catholic convent where he'd been told he was an orphan, my elder brother Rowland was summoned home to Mother at age thirteen in 1932. Since she had now remarried and assumed yet another name, Rowland asked her by what name he was supposed to be known.

'You are not Ronald Charles Brandon,' said his mother. 'Your name is Rowland Charles Marshall.'

She would give no reason why his name suddenly changed from Brandon to Marshall, nor would she explain anything about his or her past.

Over the years, when checking the records at St. Catherine's House in London, I could not find a birth or death entry for a child born January 29, 1919 under the name of Ronald Charles Brandon, whose parents, supposedly, were John and Caroline Brandon (née Hinks) of Dublin, Ireland.

That information had been provided by the Mother Generalate in her letter to me dated July 29, 1992, that the child left in the care of the convent at Littlehampton, Sussex, from 1921 to 1932, is of that name, with those parents. The father's address was recorded as Mr. John Brandon, B. Company, 56th Battalion, O Block, Portobella Barracks, Dublin, Ireland. The Mother Generalate added she was sorry to say the Sisters kept very brief records of children in those days. Further confusion in her letter is that, 'One of our older Sisters often spoke of Ronnie Marshall.' How then did the name Marshall become known to her when the child in the care of St. Joseph's convent was supposed to be named Brandon?

It is also interesting to note that the baptism of Ronald Charles Brandon held at Westminster Cathedral on 6 November, 1921, records John and Caroline Brandon as the parents. The question uppermost is how was the Cathedral able to baptize a child without a bona fide birth certificate?

After checking and re-checking the birth books held at The Greater London Record Office, covering the London areas, there was no record of this child. He simply did not exist.

In 1994 I paid another visit to my brother William in Hampshire. After a few days of settling into his home we decided to contact Mr. Lyons, Archivist of the Catholic Children's Society, who is responsible for their records held at Purley in the County of Surrey.

During our conversation over the telephone Mr. Lyons suggested we meet him at St. Joseph's, Littlehampton, Sussex, to find out if there were any useful details in their registers regarding Rowland, who had spent ten years in the care of this convent.

We arranged the day on which to visit him and caught the Waterlooville bus to Havant, at which point we then boarded a coach for Littlehampton. Lucky for us, the coach stopped close to East Street where the convent is located. We had hardly reached the wrought-iron gates, now widely opened, and noticed a crowd of people, one girl in particular who was wearing a long white dress, with a flowing white veil and decorations on her head. We discovered later the girl had recently won the title of Miss Littlehampton.

Mulling with the crowd who appeared to be walking toward a side entrance, my brother and I looked at each other, puzzled. Where was Mr. Lyons among this gathering?

Before we had time to think further, we were caught by the arm by a nun, who ushered us along with the crowd, into the chapel. On looking toward the altar, I noticed Mr. Lyons was at the front of it, down on his knees.

Having been shown a seat by the nun who disappeared as quickly as she came, William, then a heavy smoker, whispered, 'I'm off for a smoke.'

He had not been five minutes away from the chapel when the same nun officiously brought him back to his seat beside me.

'What happened?' I said.

'Oh, she caught me,' was his response.

When during mass the bell was rung three times, William chuckled and whispered, 'when I was an altar boy at St. Mary's, I rung the bell four times once instead of three times, and was given a flip round the ear by the serving priest, as we reached the sacristy.'

After mass I was somewhat surprised, when coming out of the chapel, another nun took a few guests into the library and offered us drinks. Two bishops were already in the library, partaking and downing whiskeys, in large glasses. Where, I wondered, was Mr. Lyons, whom we had planned to meet? He was nowhere in sight and throughout the function we did not see him again. Here I was being offered sherry in a glass half-filled, totally taken aback by the special treatment we were given, for what appeared out of character in a convent. In all my days I had never seen so much liquor piled on a tea-trolley, and the size of the drinks being offered was nothing short of affluence.

Then, ushered by the library nun into the dining-room, I was transfixed and glared at the amount of food on the tables, the palatial settings, white cloths, best silverware and china, and a variety of food unimaginable in my days at St. Anne's. On a long table, placed in the centre of the dining-room, was a silver tray on which stood a large iced fruit cake, made by the nuns, and beautifully decorated with the words, *Fiftieth Reunion*.

Finally, my brother and I understood the reason for the celebration of mass and the large crowds attending this special occasion, many of whom came as far away as Australia, Africa, Canada and New Zealand.

Before leaving St. Joseph's, I noticed a table in the hallway on which stood albums of photographs of some of the boys who had been at the convent. On checking to see if I would recognize one of Rowland

The old St. Anne's, demolished in the late 1970s.

I realized he would be difficult to spot, as he was unknown to me as a child.

On the return journey home to Waterlooville, William and I chatted incessantly about the day's events and were more surprised than ever to realize the sole purpose of going to Littlehampton was to meet up with Mr. Lyons, but we never had the chance to speak with him. Despite this, we both agreed it was an enjoyable outing.

This was my second visit to St. Joseph's over a two-year period. The first one I visited alone, and when meeting the Mother Generalate for the first time, she kindly invited me to stay for lunch. Two retired bishops, living in the convent, were also seated at the same dining-room table as myself. Conversation was limited. Questions by them asked about my life in Canada, to which I politely answered. I was of course tempted (by the devil) to elaborate on my childhood upbringing at St. Anne's, but being an uninvited guest decided it would be inappropriate.

After lunch, and saying goodbye to the bishops and nuns, I managed to get Mother Generalate to one side, saying, 'I've come a long way from Canada with my one goal to visit St. Joseph's and check your records of when my brother Rowland was admitted and the date he left the convent.'

Graciously, the Mother Generalate took me to an upper floor and into a small room lined with book shelves, on which were stored the convent's records. Precious few details on my brother's history were already known to me; my intention was to see if I could dig up anything further to explain why he was known as Ronnie Brandon. Alas, I found the details recorded to be contradictory.

In the Mother Generalate's letter March 23, 1991, she mentioned there appears to be no record of when Charles Brandon, son of John and Caroline Brandon, made First Communion or Confirmation or when he left. Her letter then states there is no name Ronald Brandon or Kathleen in the old records, and suggests a letter to St. George's Cathedral – 'They may be able to tell you more.'

I slipped a donation into the hand of the Mother Generalate, who waved goodbye and wished me god speed back home to Canada as she closed the front door. On my return journey from Littlehampton to William's home at Waterlooville, I felt that apart from seeing the convent where Rowland was educated, small comfort had been gained on the information of his childhood background, as their records left so many unanswered questions.

Rowland was fully aware he was brought home with the sole intent of using him, specifically as a workhorse, to supplement the family income. His homecoming was bad from the beginning. Because he was not Martin's son, the step-father had no time for the boy, much to his mother's sorrow. Rather, Martin insisted Rowland went out and worked. Wasting time reading comics was not Martin's idea of earning a living. And earn a living Rowland must, to the point that outside sports activities were strictly taboo for the step-son.

My brother recalls that when he went home, the eldest boy, Percy, was nowhere to be seen. He wasn't even aware there was another child until many years later, while searching family records, he found the boy's birth certificate. There were only two youngsters living in the house at

Carshalton, the time Rowland was brought home in 1932. The mystery surrounding the eldest son of Percy and Caroline Martin and where he was brought up, including his whereabouts are still unknown, to this day.

Because of the unfriendly atmosphere in the home, my brother, at seventeen, decided to join the Merchant Service in 1936. When saying goodbye to his mother, he told her he would be away at sea for up to two and a half years. He arranged to provide her, during the period away, with a monthly allowance from his wages, hoping it would help stretch the family budget and improve the grim relationship between his mother and step-father.

After his two-year contract expired, Rowland was eager to return home to see his mother. There was so much he had to tell her about his new experiences in the Merchant Service, and places of travel he'd only previously read about in the history books.

It was to his utter shock and dismay when arriving at Mother's house, to learn the family had moved to yet another undisclosed neighbourhood – but where, nobody knew. Despite numerous inquiries among the neighbours, to see if she had left a forwarding address, no one had any idea where she had gone. It seemed as though they had all disappeared, into a puffy cloud of oblivion.

Though he searched determinedly for decades, Rowland was never to find or see his mother again. After abandoning him when nearly three years of age, and bringing him home at thirteen, then – with total disregard for his welfare or happiness – Mother abandoned him once again before he returned home from overseas, disappearing completely without trace. No forwarding address, nothing! She appeared to have no soul, specially where her previous children were concerned. This characteristic trait of hers, so bizarre and enigmatic, would rear its ugly head again.

SECRETS REVEALED

When visiting my father's place of birth at Lydd in the County of Kent, a few years ago, I met several family members who were quite shocked to learn my father had entered into a marriage in 1915. They had no idea whatsoever he had taken a first wife!

It was so strange to them that he never thought of bringing her to meet his large family at Lydd, hence the reason for their reluctance to believe he had ever been married before. Could it be they might have objected to him marrying a girl from London, rather than one of the local girls from his own farming community?

Furthermore, none of these newly-found relatives were ever aware he had children and, until I produced a birth certificate to substantiate my claim to being his daughter, none would accept the truth. He was, to them, a man with an unblemished record, whom they held in the highest esteem.

When checking my father's two marriage certificates I noted that grandfather Edward Rutley was listed on both of them, so he must have been aware of his son's first marriage to my mother. Why then was this marriage kept so secret?

In a letter dated December 1992 from Roland Burberry, a first cousin living at Churt, Surrey, Roland said the Marshalls were a close-knit family and most honourable. He loved them all dearly and saw them all to rest. He added, how sad it was this latest news regarding his Uncle Ted's family surfaced too late as, in his mind, my father would have welcomed me in open arms.

My mother, Caroline Marshall (née Ashby).

On-going financial troubles caused my mother to move frequently, to avoid paying rent, sometimes taking what is known, as a "moonlight flit" to dodge the landlord.

With the threat of World War Two looming in 1938, she decided to move back to London and work in a 'munition factory that was put on full production in Tooting. She took with her the two small Martin children, who were eventually evacuated from London's danger zones to the quiet countryside of Cornwall when war broke out.

Having researched my mother's life over many decades and discovering to my utter dismay her murky past, I now realize what drove her to use so many alias in covering up her tracks.

When I began the arduous task of sifting through the records relating to her early life, right up until the time she passed on, I did not want to believe this one person who so deviously got away from the laws of bigamy, scot-free, was my mother. How she could live with the threat hanging over her head, realizing on any given day she could get caught? It only needed someone to start the gossip, to put her in jail. But, she did live on, and apparently with careless abandon.

Her marriage to Antonio Capolongo, who was of the Catholic faith, opened a door for her. Taking full advantage of the situation she blatantly used the Catholic Church and its institutions, to rid herself of her children. No doubt she gave stories that held hardly a grain of truth. Consider the fact that in every record, her religious creed was shown to be that of the Church of England. Yet, over and over, when questioning various priests in London why she was allowed to have five of her children baptized in Catholic churches, their response was always, 'Unless she herself was a practicing Catholic, it was unlikely the children could be baptized as Catholics.' Yet, for some reason, this did not apply in my mother's case. Perhaps she gave them such a convincing story about her children's plight, the Churchmen felt it was important to save the children's souls, if nothing else.

The marriage certificate between Caroline Florence Hinks and John Brandon dated December 17, 1919 shows John Brandon senior (deceased) and Joseph Hinks senior (deceased). Was this a mere co-incidence, or a cover-up? The marriage was clearly bigamous, as at this time she was married in 1915 to Edward Rutley Pocock Marshall, who did not divorce her until 1926.

Referring back to a document received from the Greater London Record Office, at the time of my birth when my mother entered Walworth Institution on September 21, 1925, she gave her occupation as 'Wardrobe Dealer'. She was thirty-seven years of age.

When entering into the 1919 marriage with John Brandon, Caroline Florence Hinks was recorded as a spinster, thirty-one years of age, described as a 'Wardrobe Dealer'. Her year of birth would be 1888 – the same as Caroline Marshall (née Ashby).

The names Ada Florence were those given to her eldest sister. Both sisters looked very much alike, although apparently they appeared to have little in common. Perhaps this was the reason why my mother used the name "Florence" as her middle name, to avoid her own identification being discovered.

On many of my visits to London, after emigrating to Canada in 1967, I headed directly to St. Catherine's House in London to search through the heavy volumes of births, marriages and deaths, looking for any clue relating to either of my parents. This is an arduous task in itself, where desk space on which to place the volumes, is limited. Many researchers give up trying for desktop space and end up sitting on the floor, with the volumes spread out in front of them.

The volumes are extremely heavy to handle, and after a tiring day of lifting and putting them back onto their appropriate shelves, one returns home with aching muscles and a stiffness that last for days. If a researcher finds the smallest piece of the information for which they are looking, a day at St. Catherine's can be quite rewarding. On the other hand, it can also bring home the sheer misery and frustration in not finding exactly what one is searching.

Checking and rechecking fervently as ever over the years, despite all my efforts, I could not trace a Caroline Florence Hinks born 1888, in either the birth or death records. Therefore I came to the conclusion that this person simply did not exist. In my estimation, unquestionably, Caroline Marshall (née Ashby) and Caroline Florence Brandon (née Hinks) were one and the same woman. But this didn't dawn on me until decades of searching, when I finally put together the pieces of her life.

Sifting through endless piles of paperwork gathered over forty-odd years, I could map out the sordid details of her four marriages. Having found no proof she was divorced from Antonio Capolongo, her first husband, one can only assume her following three marriages were bigamous. The records show that the first five of her children were institutionalized at an early age. When all the dirt was uncovered I still would not believe this was my mother who resorted to such a scandalous lifestyle, the likes of which would be regarded as unimaginable in most decent families.

When I mentioned to the late Angus Baxter I had finally come to the realization that this one person who had created such agonies in the lives of her children, was my mother, and who was known both as Ashby and Hinks, his comment was, 'I could have told you that, but I wanted you to find out for yourself.'

Not wishing to be too harsh, in a letter to Angus, I wrote, 'How could anyone do this to a family?'

To which he replied, 'She was a lusty, loving woman, who did things her way.'

I couldn't argue with that!

With the failure of my mother's marriages, she had no prospects of a decent life, due to self-destruction and lack of respect. While the records show her firstborn, named Marie, passed away at sixteen months of age, we still cannot determine if her marriage to Antonio Capolongo was annulled, thereby allowing her legally to enter into a marriage with Edward Rutley Pocock Marshall, Chief Petty Officer of the Royal Navy.

Their son Rowland, whom she conveniently abandoned at three years of age to a convent, under an assumed name, was brought home at the age of thirteen. She then disappeared from his life without trace, when he returned to England after a two-year contract with the Merchant Service. Her second son and three other daughters were put into orphanages until old enough to go "out into the world" on their own. She made no effort to ever contact them. Might she have thought they were better off not knowing her?

During her fourth marriage to Percy Martin, with whom she had three sons, the whereabouts of her eldest son remains to this day a mystery. He was not seen in the household when my eldest brother Rowland went to stay with Mother in 1932. The on-going questions: where is he, was he hidden away in some orphanage to later sign on a ship and start a new life overseas? Having checked all UK records, there is no trace of him.

My mother's life was definitely not an easy one; her appetite for the good life eventually led to her downfall. In 1952, following a serious stomach operation, she passed away at the age of sixty-four at Margate in the County of Kent. She was buried in St. John's Church cemetery.

FULL CIRCLE

If someone was to ask the question: *knowing what you know today, would you do the years of research all over again?* my answer would have to be *yes*. The drive to know my roots was so intense that I was determined, regardless of whatever hurdles I had to cross, not to allow anyone or anything stand in my way.

Had I been aware of The Society of Genealogists headquarters in London when I began my search in 1944, I'm sure I would not have travelled trails, long cold, in all the wrong places. The back and forth exhausting journeys to the East End of London left me physically drained, and I wondered many times if I would have the strength to continue, alone, the search for my parents. Often, walking many miles through bombed-out London, I would stop to rest, sitting on a pile of debris, with dust and dirt everywhere. If lucky enough to be able to purchase a piece of fruit for sixpence from a barrow boy, this I considered was lunch; the only food I ate throughout the day.

As far as the Catholic authorities were concerned, I should not have wasted my time in trying to extract from them information; the 'silent rule' prevailed, no matter what! It is only with recent changes in the laws that those children who were put under their charge, have found the information that they searched for. Sadly, for many of us it has come all too late, and has caused needless misery to those who have lived a lifetime, alone, and without family.

In a letter from Mr. M. Lyons of the Catholic Children's Society in Purley, Surrey, dated June 14, 1993, he wrote, 'Yes, it is sad that it has taken so long for people like yourself to locate families. It is really only since 1976 when adoption records were opened up for the first time that it had become so evident to everyone, how important family records are. The expertise in tracing is fairly recent and we have learned so much in recent years about what is available, where to look, and how to "prise" information out of the archives of long-defunct Agencies.

'As you have already gathered, there was no co-ordinated Welfare Service for children much before the 1950s, and certainly few professionally-trained people with any knowledge of child development or needs. The old orphanages just provided the basic minimum in shelter, food, clothing and education but could not by the very nature of the institutions provide anything in the way of real individual love or meet the individual emotional needs of young children. Even today the authorities are "struggling" to find answers to complex questions of why some families survive and others cannot cope.'

Throughout my correspondence with Mr. Lyons, going back to October 1988, I must say in all honesty that in all my inquiries concerning my childhood background, he has made a thorough search of the records, currently held at Purley in the County of Surrey, England, and given me details that were perhaps useful or beneficial to me, relating to my two sisters and myself.

There was, however, one particular letter I received from him dated September 11, 1989, which was in response to an inquiry concerning my brother William, who had been put under the care of the Sisters of Charity nuns at Gravensend in the County of Kent.

After searching, he had eventually found an entry in an old register held at St. Mary's, but it gave little knowledge, other than the date he was admitted, his first Communion, Confirmation, and when discharged. There was, however, a piece of information which both William and I were totally unaware of, up to this time, and I was so angry when reading these details, I could have exploded: 'Nearest relative mother, Caroline, 105 Albany Flats, Albany Road, Peckham, London. This is then crossed through and underneath is written No.72 Westminster Bridge Road, London.'

It was, without doubt, an appalling thing for the Catholic authorities to withhold this, after begging them since the mid-1940s to give us any details, however small, to enable us to find Mother. For years they kept this vital piece of information to themselves, saying repeatedly, 'We don't know.'

The knowledge I now have of my family's history has enabled me to get to the bottom of exactly what happened in my early life and that of my mother. This awareness has given me profound relief from so much pent-up self-doubt and worry – in sharp contrast to the philosophy of the Catholic authorities still ringing in my ears, 'what you don't know, you won't miss, so let sleeping dogs lie.'

Of course I am left wondering if the long journeys I had made from Canada to visit Surrey, Kent and London, in the search of my parents over many years, were worthwhile. Ironically, I was so close to finding them, visiting both parts of their world, but when I finally discovered where they lived, they had already passed on.

Having come full circle, and realizing a goal which appeared insurmountable, I can now look back on the past forty years of researching as being the most challenging experience of my life. I have met many people willing to help a complete stranger in the smallest way and, when travelling around the East End of London, exploring dark, narrow corners, which terrified me, I found the Cockney, East Enders, the most warm-hearted, endearing characters of them all. When asking for information as to how I could get to a specific area, such as the Catholic Church of the English Martyrs, or other areas of Walworth, a Cockney would sometimes go out of his way and take me directly to the place where I was heading, chatting all the way, and laughing in the good-humorous manner that only a Cockney knows best. Leaving me at my destination, he would shout, 'Good luck, ducks,' as he disappeared in the opposite direction, waving madly as he went on his way.

My roots, now firmly established, have come to light through the generosity of the late Angus Baxter, who gave me his invaluable time and advice so freely on where, or how to go about extracting information from the various Record Offices and Government departments in England. To him I owe a debt so great, it can never be repaid. But for the doors he "opened", it would have been an impossible task for me to secure my father's service records from the Ministry of Defence, and also my parents' birth, marriage and death certificates through Mr. Rudall, his contact in London.

My greatest joy when Mr. Baxter wrote telling me that he had found my family, was that once contact had been made with them, photographs on both sides of the family were made available to me.

On one of my visits to the tiny village of Lydd in the County of Kent, I visited Jim Cobley, a relative who was kind enough to invite me into his home. We talked at great length about the family of Marshalls, who had lived at Lydd for many generations.

I asked Jim if he was in possession of any photographs of my father and grandfather, for I was desperate to see what they looked like, though realizing that one cannot always judge a person by an image one sees. He left the room and when he returned he handed me a large cardboard shoe box that had been stored away in a cupboard, for many years, which contained numerous family portraits. As I studied this large collection of photographs of family members whom I was aware of but had never seen, I couldn't believe my good fortune.

I was delighted when Jim said, 'Take whatever pictures you want. I'll be happy to give them to you.'

I looked hard at two of the pictures of my father in his Navy uniform and knew these were the ones I wanted, also those of his sisters and parents.

One photograph of him was one taken of the ship's company aboard the *HMS Dragon* in 1919, in front of Toronto's City Hall, when the Prince of Wales was visiting Canada. It's an historical picture, which I was happy to accept.

Throughout the course of my search for my roots, whatever information became known to me, along with any photographs I was able to extract from living relatives, copies of all these documents were forwarded to my brother William and sisters, Margaret and Elizabeth, so they were kept completely up-to-date with current news and progress I had made.

Grandmother Ashby had six daughters and four sons, two of whom died at a very young age. These children have, unfortunately, all passed on by the time we discovered them. Uncle Ernest, one of my mother's

My father, Edward Rutley Pocock Marshall,
Royal Navy, at 23 years of age.

brothers, whom I had been trying to trace passed away February, 1989, just months before I determined his whereabouts. His wife Phyllis died in 1992.

Of the children of my uncles and aunts, some live in Australia, New Zealand, Quebec in Canada, and England. There is some mystery attached to my Aunt Lilian Ashby and her second husband, John O'Connor, whose child Marie O'Connor was also born at 182 Westmoreland Road, Walworth, and appears to have been taken to Canada by her father many years ago. Decades have been spent trying to trace her whereabouts, to no avail.

My brother William passed away at eight-three years of age in 2007 and is buried alongside his late wife, Violet, at Winchester, Hampshire, England. He served in the Royal Navy for twenty-seven years and retired on a Navy pension. On one of his seafaring trips, William heroically saved his ship when the engine room caught fire. He was awarded the Bravery Medal. With three children, the eldest son living in Michigan, USA, William had ten grandchildren.

My sister Margaret married a young soldier named William Evans, who served in the Canadian Army during World War Two. In 1947 she sailed to Canada with other war brides, and lived with her husband in Quebec. A young child was born to them; however, sadly, the baby died of a crib death. To add further to her anguish, her husband drowned a few days later while swimming in a lake. Such a tragedy my sister never got over. After many years of struggling to maintain herself in Canada she decided to emigrate to the United States, but her life here has been far from easy. Her love of animals far exceeds that of the human race. Despite the extreme hardships Margaret has endured throughout her life, she can still come up smiling. Like the rest of us, she is a true survivor.

My younger sister Elizabeth, a most endearing, loving person who wouldn't hurt a living thing, after a lifetime of looking after the young, old and sick, was hanging on to life by a thin thread before passing away in 1993. Her death left an enormous gap in my life. We were sisters and close friends and I loved her dearly. A devout Catholic, she never questioned the Church's theology, and stood by her faith resolutely.

Of all the frustrations throughout my search for family, the one "fly in the ointment" has to be John Brandon, an Irishman who was one of mother's four husbands. He was born in Dublin in 1890. On July 4, 1910, he joined the Royal Navy as a Stoker II Class on a 12-year engagement. On July 3, 1922, he was released ashore from *HMS Victory II*, the period of his continuous service having expired. He joined the Royal Fleet Reserve on October 20, 1924.

In a letter from the Ministry of Defence dated July 10, 1991 responding to an inquiry on Brandon's service records, it stated: 'We have established that he was released from the Royal Fleet Reserve in November 1932 and we have every confidence that he did not serve in the Royal Navy during World War II; certainly he did not die on active service with the Royal Navy during that conflict. Further research has shown that, whilst his service record gives his previous occupation as "Ship Fitter's Mate", his engagement papers show him to have been a "Farm Labourer". Which is odd, and that he had previously served with the Third Battalion, Scottish Rifles (Special Reserve), although he enlisted in the Royal Navy in Belfast.'

In a further letter dated September 30, 1991 from the Ministry of Defence, it stated: 'In reply to your enquiry, we regret that no records relating to the Military service of 40123 Peter John Brandon or John Brandon, Scottish Rifles, in the British Army during the 1914–18 war can now be traced. Unfortunately, as was mentioned in our original letter, a large proportion of the records of soldiers who served during the period 1914–1920 were totally destroyed by enemy air action in 1940 and it would seem that those of the above-named were among them.'

In reply to my letter of June 2, 1992 to The Camerons (Scottish Rifles), Chester, England, their response was negative, but they did furnish me with some background information relating to this battalion, which I found most interesting: 'The Third Special Reserve Battalion came into being as a consequence of Lord Haldane's Army reforms of 1908. During the Great War the battalion was mobilized and was sent to Nigg in Ross-shire, Scotland, where it remained until 1918 when it proceeded to Invergordon, and the following year to Bridge of Allan. When trouble in Ireland became acute, the Battalion moved to Curragh. It may be that during their stay there, your relative left the Regiment and joined the Royal Navy.'

Because of the destruction of Dublin records in 1922, it is impossible to secure the birth certificate of John Brandon. The one and only record I have relating to him is the marriage certificate of December 17, 1919, when he and my mother married in a London Registry Office. Even this document is questionable.

My father's body was cremated at Charing in the County of Kent, in January of 1958, and my mother buried at St. John's Cemetery, Margate, in April of 1952. These districts were within close proximity to one another. Ironically, in the 1950s, my sister Elizabeth had worked in the Margate area, never realizing how close she was to her mother.

When Rowland and I visited Mother's grave in 1992 it was on a bitterly cold day and, as we walked from the railway station along the beach front, the wind and rain howled across from the ocean, causing large waves to splash unmercifully over the shoreline. With the help of our taxi driver who took us from the town area to the cemetery, there we were able to find a stone with a discreet number, where she was laid to rest. We stood by the graveside for a few minutes, deep in thought, that perhaps life might have been so different had we known of her whereabouts before she passed away.

Despite our ups and downs, I keep in touch with the rest of my family. We all care about each other, perhaps more so than those siblings who had parents to nurture their every need, especially love. To us, brought up in the harsh discipline of an orphanage, we have overcome the ordeal, with a little scarring, and survived the many shadows. For an orphaned child alone and shivering in a dormitory bed, merely seeing the shadow of a nun approaching evoked such terror as to create a lifetime memory.

As Mr. Lyons of the Catholic Children's Society emphasized, authorities today are still struggling to find answers why some families survive and others cannot cope. I am still in touch with several "old girls" from St. Anne's and it would appear sadly that most of them have had disastrous marriages, to the point were they have been physically abused by their husbands. Yet, in order to survive, most decided to "tolerate their lot".

As one friend put it to me: 'I didn't want to lose my children, which might have happened if I left my husband, and have them ending up with complete strangers, as happened to me as a child. So did the best I could with a disastrous marriage.'

I have always tried to envisage my parents' plight in their marriage and do not wish to judge them too harshly for allowing my brothers, sisters and me to be put into institutions. It was bad enough being born in one, let alone being brought up in one. Although the pain hurts, I try not to dwell on it, as after all we have much to be thankful for in that we now know who we are, and where we come from. Both sides of our family were honourable people; they were not responsible for the depression years, when families were destitute and unable to clothe and feed their children.

There are, of course, many questions that can never be resolved. Some mysteries surrounding the complexities of our background were known only to Mother, who unfortunately has taken her secrets to the grave.

Her first husband, an Italian named Antonio Capolongo, to whom she married at the age of twenty-one in 1910, and their daughter Marie born in 1911, who passed away at sixteen months.

The mysterious John Brandon, no records! How could it be possible for Mother to have married this man in 1919 when she was already married to Edward Rutley Pocock Marshall in 1915, and who did not divorce her until 1926? It is difficult to comprehend she was married to both men at the same time and yet, the records show this could be the case. Could this person calling herself Caroline Florence Hinks be Mother, or – a wild theory – is it perhaps Ada Florence Ashby who had married Brandon and the families have been mixed up? My instinct tells me this is not so.

In a letter dated June 1993 from my first cousin living in Sussex, England, she remembers, '… as a child, hearing the name of Brandon but cannot relate to whom or by whom; also the name Hinks rings a bell which seems very familiar but again cannot remember why. It may have been with your mother's sister Ada, but?'

Over the past years I have been delving for information in the Genealogy Library at the Church of the Latter Day Saints in Victoria, who have a vast network of family records. One day I asked one of the many knowledgeable librarians why the Church was so keen on family history.

Her reply was, 'If you don't know your family history and your roots, you will never know yourself.'

I was impressed by this piece of sound philosophy which, whilst true, it did not appear to be considered important enough or come within

My brother, Rowland Charles Marshall,
who lived with me in Canada after his wife died.

the scope of the Catholic theologians to adopt this same philosophy with regard to the birthright of those children under their care. It might have been, for many of us, a different lifestyle in our adult years had we been given the choice when discharged from the orphanage, to be told our identity and family background. At least be given a birth certificate, albeit in some cases, a false one. This, unfortunately, was not the case for the children who were put into St. Anne's.

Having studied the history written about St. Anne's over the years, I was not surprised to learn that over 5,000 young children from the orphanages were shipped out to Irish-Canadian homes in Canada in the early 1900s, to work as domestic servants and farm labourers.

To come full circle, it truly is a miracle to have found our elder brother Rowland, at seventy-two years of age, alive, having miraculously survived when his ship was torpedoed during World War II. After a lifetime of family searching, we have in our possession photographs of our parents, as well as other family members. Following the death of his wife Gladys in 1990, Rowland moved to Canada. After my husband died in 1999,

Rowland lived with me until his death in 2008, a few months after his 89th birthday. His last public appearance was a book signing event for the launch of his memoirs *Luck Was My Companion: Adventures of an Old Sea Dog*. Rowland is survived by a son and daughter, five grandchildren and two great-grandchildren.

Sharing a home with my brother for many years finally gave me a rich sense of what "family life" together as children might have been like. Knowing our connections to the Marshalls and Ashbys, my brothers, sisters and I were content in the knowledge that what we have discovered about them is, without a shadow of doubt, the truth. Although we are still puzzled with a few of the details surrounding the family history, we realize some of the mystery concerning Mother will forever remain. This is something we have come to terms with, and accepted. Having survived many hardships during our lives, we have been able to tell this true story of siblings who, through sheer willpower despite many hurdles to cross, were determined to achieve their goal in finding their roots.

ABOUT THE AUTHOR

Caroline Whitehead (née Marshall) was born in London, England. Abandoned in infancy, she was brought up as an orphan in a Catholic institution in a small village in the County of Kent. On reaching the age of sixteen she was sent out into a world she knew little of, as a domestic servant. With World War Two in progress she was soon conscripted into an aircraft factory in the County of Surrey, on 'munition work. She married in 1944.

When hostilities ended, she enrolled in a commercial college to train as a secretary. After emigrating to Canada in 1967, a long emotional journey began as she regularly travelled between England and Canada over the years, in a desperate attempt to learn the truth about her parents, and find her missing family.

Caroline has one child, three grandchildren and two great-grandchildren. She lives in British Columbia, Canada.

CPSIA information can be obtained at www.ICGtesting.com
Printed in the USA
LVOW12s1845230813

349025LV00005BA/16/P

9 781897 435335